Principles
of
Progression

Principles
of
Progression

by Kevin Stott

BONNEVILLE BOOKS™
Springville, Utah

ISBN: 1-55517-656-9
v.1

Published by Bonneville Books
Imprint of Cedar Fort Inc.
www.cedarfort.com

Distributed by:

Typeset by Kristin Nelson
Cover design by Adam Ford
Cover design © 2002 by Lyle Mortimer

Printed in the United States of America
10 9 8 7 6 5 4 3 2 1

Printed on acid-free paper

Library of Congress Cataloging-in-Publication Data

Stott, Kevin, 1954-
  Principles of progression / by Kevin Stott.
    p. cm.
  ISBN 1-55517-656-9 (pbk.)
  1. Christian life--Mormon authors. 2. Church of Jesus Christ of
Latter-day Saints--Doctrines. I. Title.
  BX8656 .S76 2002
  248.4'89332--dc21
                    2002006731

Table of Contents

Chapter 1

The Principle of Progression

When I had been out in the mission field a mere two weeks, my companion, Elder Jensen, asked me to cut his hair. Since he had just cut my hair I felt an obligation to return the favor, although it was against my better instincts. I expressed concerns to him about my lack of skill in the barbering trade, but he reassured me that if I followed his instructions that I would do a fine job. After listening to him discourse upon the fundamentals of haircutting, I diffidently picked up a lock of hair and carefully chopped it off. I winced as I made the cut, frightened that I might have done something immutably wrong—fully aware that once the hair was gone there was nothing I could do to restore it.

After a few minutes of uncertain hacking, my confidence began to swell. My snips with the scissors became more precise and defined. Soon I was gathering tight bundles of hair in my left hand and with deft strokes of my right hand skillfully mowed them to the ground. The job was progressing nicely. I enjoyed the task. I whistled as I worked. Finally, I stepped back from my client to observe what I had done and was well pleased with the effect. It was quite obvious that I possessed a natural aptitude for barbering.

I resumed my work. I grabbed a hunk of hair on the front of his head and with one decisive stroke of the scissors irretrievably reduced it to a pile of protein on the floor. Alas, something was dreadfully wrong. I stepped back once more. The fine effect of my companion's coiffure had disappeared.

His appearance had been radically altered. Somehow I had whacked off all of his bangs, creating a highly-visible bald spot right above his eyes.

I began to nervously and uncontrollably giggle. A glimmer of anxiety appeared faintly in my companion's eyes and was reflected in the tremulous quality of his voice as he asked the cause of my behavior. "Oh, nothing is wrong," I assured him, "or at least permanently wrong. Someday you won't even remember I gave you a haircut."

My words failed to inspire him with the necessary confidence, and he leaped hastily off the chair and rushed to the bathroom to gaze at himself in the mirror. I knew that he had reached it when he began to scream, moan, and act completely undignified. To alleviate his vain concerns, I sagely pointed out that at least now he wouldn't have hair falling in his eyes, obscuring his vision.

In this temporal world, which we co-inhabit with Satan and his minions, our vision can easily be obscured behind a screen of darkness. So pervasive is Satan's sinister influence on this planet, that, according to the scriptures, the whole world groans in darkness, and gross darkness covers the eyes of the people of this earth. These prevailing societal conditions can readily obscure our own vision, and in this murky light, decisions that appear worldly-wise, are, in fact, eternally stupid.

Fortunately, there is a countervailing power upon this earth, a power of such refulgent light that even the blind can see out of obscurity and darkness. The truth that is in Christ is a light that shines with such intensity that it can penetrate even the blackest abyss of sin and hell. Ultimately, those who have cloaked themselves behind the shielding anonymity of worldly philosophy will see with perfect clarity the individual consequences of their actions. There is no ambiguity to our decisions when under the full glare of the light shining from the Son of God.

The Savior said:

"And that which doth not edify is not of God, and is darkness.

"That which is of God is light; and he that receiveth light, and continueth in God, receiveth more light; and that light groweth brighter and brighter until the perfect day" (D&C 50:23-24).

We came to this earth endowed with a spirit. God is the father of our spirits, and through him we inherit the characteristics of Godliness. As a reminder of this spiritual lineage, every person born in mortality is also endowed with the light of Christ. The light of Christ is truth, and shines as a beacon of progression for those who willingly seek the light. Innate within every human being is this yearning for progression. The principle of progression encompasses three contiguous stages: knowledge, then goodness, then faith.

In 1974 I was in Norfolk, Virginia tracting with a rookie missionary companion. Elder Anderson had been in the mission field less than a month, and still found tracting an exhilarating experience. We knocked on a door in an upscale neighborhood. We were greeted by a well-dressed, grey-haired lady who immediately invited us in before we could make a door approach. We walked into the front room and sat down on the couch. Every available space in the room was occupied by a bouquet of flowers. I recognized that something unusual was going on, and before my neophyte companion could launch into a full-scale missionary invasion I fired off a few questions to determine the "lay of the land."

The answers to my questions revealed that we had walked into the home of a man who had died two days previously. The grief-stricken lady we were talking to was his sister from out of town who had come to settle his affairs. It became obvious to us that she assumed we were two young pastors from his church coming to comfort her. Having inadvertently accepted this mistaken identity, we were not sure how to shake it. Under the doleful influence of our surroundings, we chose instead to remain incognito and offer some measure of hope to this disconsolate lady, even though we were not her brother's spiritual ministers.

Accordingly, we presented a series of consoling platitudes such as, "he is so much happier now, he's in a far better place, he's no longer suffering." Our expressions must have aroused her suspicions because she began asking us specific questions concerning her brother. In the name of altruism, we found ourselves scrambling evasively out of the quicksand and into the mire. After a few minutes of receiving our evasive replies she gave up and directed me to pray for the deceased. Since I was still ignorant of his name, this turned out to be an extremely awkward assignment. Somehow I managed to get through a properly solicitous benediction, after which we made an appropriately rapid exit.

From the Doctrine and Covenants we learn this:

"And truth is knowledge of things as they are, and as they were, and as they are to come..." (D&C 93:24).

Ignorance of truth is damning, while a knowledge of the truth is an essential element in becoming like God. Truth is eternal, and encompasses that broad spectrum of understanding that created the earth and all things on it. Things that are true will edify and enlighten our minds, causing us to see clearly the opposing forces of good and evil. A knowledge of the plan of salvation and its requirements is the most critical information that we can assimilate into our minds during this brief mortal span.

By contrast, accepting false teachings and worldly practices as a convenient expedient to excel in a materialistic environment, obscures our spiritual vision and diminishes our ability to think and act like God. Trying to please Christ while appeasing Satan creates a spiritual dichotomy. No matter how hard we try, we cannot serve two masters. At some point in time, we must position ourselves squarely on the side of truth and righteousness.

Many years ago, the University of Arizona experimental farm owned a registered Holstein bull of exceptional quality. I cannot recall his official pedigreed name, but he was called Tidy. Tidy was a huge beast, weighing more than a ton. His confirmation was nearly perfect, and he won every blue ribbon at every show he entered. As physically impressive as Tidy was, he carried one noticeable flaw: he was mean of temperament and extremely dangerous. His pen was constructed with three-inch-thick iron pipe, which bulged out in several places, mute testimony to his colossal strength and irascible temper.

Many years later, I came to know a cow by the name of Lucy. Lucy was a nondescript bovine of uncertain ancestry. She was brown and white with peculiar markings and a crooked horn sticking out one side of her head. She was beefy and squat, and lacked the angularity and sharpness so prized in a dairy animal. But Lucy was different in another way as well. Unlike most of her 800 other herdmates, she was perfectly gentle and good-natured. She patiently stood to be scratched or patted, and reciprocated all displays of affection by licking faces with her sandpaper rough tongue. The milkers often jumped on her back when driving the cows to the milking parlor, and like a well-broke saddle horse she would give them a safe ride.

There are two contrasting beauties in life: One is the beauty of physical form called *pulchritude*. The other is the beauty of the soul called *goodness*. One is centered on pride and selfishness, the other on humility and selflessness. One is spiritually retrogressive, the other eternally progressive.

The root of the word *good* is *God*. To be good is to be like

God. The active characteristics of Godliness are virtue and charity. To be virtuous and charitable is to be benevolent and kind, tender, compassionate, self-controlled. It is to be patient and understanding, generous in giving, magnanimously forgiving. Compressed in meaning, to be good is to love one another as God loves us, and to treat one another as Christ treated others. As we progress in goodness, we progress toward Godliness.

When I was a small boy my family lived in a secure little neighborhood in Tucson, Arizona. In our backyard was a large sandbox. Behind our sandbox stood an ancient Eucalyptus tree. This tree stood sentinel over our entire back yard, and from the top of its immense height could be seen the busy activities of several neighborhoods. Because of its potential for expanding my seven-year-old horizons, I decided one day to climb high into the Eucalyptus tree.

Our home was situated so that the kitchen window looked out upon the backyard. From her position at the kitchen sink my mother could look out the window and keep a wary eye upon her brood of six children. On this fateful day, she was busy peeling potatoes for dinner while taking an occasional glance outside to check on the status of her kids. Because her attention was diverted for a few minutes she did not see me get a chair and boost myself up on the lowest branch of the Eucalyptus tree. From the lowest branch I ascended higher, and although it made me giddy to look down, I enjoyed the thrill of seeing the world from so high a perspective.

My enthusiasm for the new vistas below me engendered a desire on my part to share some of the excitement that I was feeling. Looking down, I spotted my mother standing at the kitchen sink diligently scrubbing potatoes. Tightly grabbing a branch with my two little fists, I began to swing back and forth while yelling at my mom to attract her attention. Hearing a commotion, she looked up. Her eyes quickly scanned the backyard, mentally checking off the whereabouts of her children. A movement caught her eye and she glanced up and saw me swinging back and forth high in the Eucalyptus tree. The shock of seeing me in such a precarious position was too much for her. She keeled over in a dead faint. To this day she is the only woman to have ever swooned over me.

To progress in faith requires us to climb higher and higher on the branches of knowledge and goodness. Climbing higher by faith is always accompanied by a certain degree of risk; the higher we climb the more dangerous the fall. The laws of spiritual physics state that positive ascension toward heaven is always opposed by the gravitational pull of hell. As we learn the things we should do, and as we do the things we learn, our faith propels us beyond the static grip of sin and into the stratosphere of virtue. Climbing the tree of life with faith expands our perspective and enables us to see the wide expanse of eternity far beyond the narrow boundaries of our mortal existence.

We were sent to earth with the singular objective to become like God. Inherent within each man and woman is the potential for divine progression through the light of Christ. As we seek this light, we acquire a knowledge of truth. As we add to our knowledge, we acquire goodness. As we add to our goodness, we acquire faith and come to a full realization of our divine possibilities.

Chapter 2

Windows of Opportunity

It was a peaceful summer afternoon in southern Utah. I was lounging at my sister's house reading a book and gazing out a window at the valley below. My kids were outside playing with their cousins and my wife was visiting with her father. This was an idyllic vacation: peace and quiet, an intriguing book, a soft couch, and no ringing phones. For a few brief minutes, all was right with the world.

My solitude was momentarily interrupted by my sister, who entered the room and offered me an apple. She believed in the adage that an apple a day keeps the physician away. I accepted her offer and began to munch my way to robust health. Finding the apple too mellow for my palate, I decided that good health from proper nutrition was highly overrated and looked for a way to dispose of the portion I had not eaten. Since I found myself reluctant to break the state of laziness I had not worked so hard to achieve, I scanned the room for a trash can. When my inspection availed nothing I mentally went in search of an alternative dumping site.

My mind was drawn to the prospects of throwing the apple through the open window, past the balcony, and down the hill upon which the house was built. The temptation grew as I realized that no one would be aware of my action and the apple would soon decompose under the influence of the desert sun. The challenge would be to throw with sufficient force to clear the balcony railing and the yard below. Glancing over my book to see whether anyone was nearby to detect my movements, with one lightning thrust I hurled the apple towards the open window. My carefully-crafted plan would have worked perfectly—if the window had actually been open!

As mortal beings endowed with agency, we are unrestrained as to the choice of those windows of opportunity which appear open to us. In a world filled with deception, we must be constantly vigilant that our choices are not wasted on windows that appear to be open but which, in actuality, are closed to eternal possibilities. The prophet Nephi described those windows in these words:

> "And there shall also be many which shall say: Eat, drink, and be merry; nevertheless, fear God—he will justify in committing a little sin; yea, lie a little, take the advantage of one because of his words, dig a pit for thy neighbor; there is no harm in this; and do all these things, for tomorrow we die; and if it so be that we are guilty, God will beat us with a few stripes, and at last we shall be saved in the kingdom of God" (2 Ne. 28:8).

While these enticing words are appealing to the irresolute natural man who desires spiritual immunity from his temporal activities, they are like closed windows which offer no hope of a celestial breeze behind their glass facade. Such teachings close off real opportunities by lulling us into a spiritual sleep filled with complacent dreams that all is well.

By contrast, the Savior's teachings invite us to awaken to the spiritual opportunities offered by adherence to his plan. He knows that once we fall prey to the seductive philosophies of the world we severely limit our future choices and waste that mortal commodity in shortest supply—the element of time.

> "For behold, this life is the time for men to prepare to meet God; yea, behold the day of this life is the day for men to perform their labors" (Alma 34:32).

Time spent on the frivolous and vain things of the world does us dual disservice. Not only have we squandered valuable opportunities to acquire truth, and thus liberate us from the bonds of sin, we have also diverted our minds and hearts away from God and placed them on man-made idols. It is the outcome of this battle over the allegiance of our minds and hearts that will ultimately determine our eternal destiny.

"Behold, the Lord requireth the heart and a willing mind; and the willing and obedient shall eat the good of the land of Zion in these last days" (D&C 64:34).

One brisk spring morning my son and I rode our horses up into the hills east of our small Idaho town. The sun was out, but a stiff breeze robbed us of its warmth. Along the trail, someone had polluted the landscape by dumping trash. The wind caused the garbage to flap up and down unpredictably. As our horses rounded a bend in the trail and were suddenly confronted by this disconcerting flapping, they reacted by fleeing away from what appeared to them to be an inexplicable danger.

Undoubtedly we would have arrived at a much different destination than the one intended had our horses been allowed to entertain their fears and exercise their desires. By using hand and leg cues they had been trained to accept, we redirected their minds so that they willingly moved in the direction we wanted them to go.

The trail leading to our celestial destination is littered with disconcerting and diverting trash, and if we do not rein in our desires and fears when they are aroused, we are apt to end up at the wrong kingdom. Yielding our will to God at times when we feel defiant is the supreme test for entry into His eternal world. Those who pass this rigorous test of character consecration discover that the windows of heaven are open to them, and that from those open windows a beneficent Father in Heaven pours out blessings upon His children.

God's blessings are uniquely customized for our individual growth and development, based on his understanding of our spiritual needs and our inclination for spiritual mischief. He knows our weaknesses, and his blessings are scheduled to buttress thin lines of defense. As we exercise our faith in God and humble ourselves before him, we come to the startling realization that our idea of what constitutes a spiritual benefice and his thoughts concerning the same subject may not be identical. While his objective for us is centered on eternal life, our expectations from him are usually more mundane.

"For all who will have a blessing at my hands shall abide the law which was appointed for that blessing, and the conditions thereof, as were instituted from before the foundation of the world" (D&C 132:5).

Is it possible that we do not receive our requested blessings because they are based on terrestrial concerns, which are not covered by preordained law?

It is unlikely that any contingency of mortal existence would be overlooked in the preexistent councils. Certainly all earthly matters would be efficiently organized under the broad umbrella of eternal law. James, the brother of Jesus, tells us that the reason we do not receive sought-after blessings has to do with the nature of the request and its intended usage.

"Ye ask, and receive not, because ye ask amiss, that ye may consume it upon your lusts" (James 4:3).

In our mortal condition we cannot escape the concerns of earth life. To remain on this earth during the time allotted our probation requires us to provide for the necessities of temporal existence, including food, clothing, and shelter. It would appear that these temporal blessings are a necessary antecedent for the reception of spiritual blessings, the one in its legitimate use foreshadowing the other. As we recognize with appreciation the source of our earthly blessings, we become sensitive to the more subtle workings of the Spirit, which ultimately guides us in truth's path towards the higher principles framed under celestial law.

Chapter 3

Peace Through Sanctification

It was midnight, the witching hour, and although the air was hot and sultry I was peacefully descending into the world of sleep when something in the waking world attached itself to my shoulder and demanded attention. After struggling with consciousness, I finally realized my wife was suggesting to me that there was a problem outside in the barnyard, that she could hear the water pump cycling continuously. Shrugging off the effects of sleep, I dragged myself out of bed and stumbled out the back door to investigate.

Outside under the stars, the August night was fragrant with dust and cow manure. I, too, could hear the water pump laboring to deliver water to the various troughs, and since that was abnormal, I began to search to see if any of the connecting lines had been broken or disconnected. As I approached the weaned-calves' pen, I could see that the hose carrying water to their trough had been severed from its connection and was running full stream. While I puzzled over the cause of this peculiarity, I heard a noise and turned my head to the north. Standing fifteen feet away was a large Holstein bull, one of 150 that we raise annually at our feedlot. Behind him stood another bull, and down the feed alley I could dimly make out two or three others.

In our business we firmly believe in the power of a bull. Because of their prodigious strength, a yearling Holstein bull is capable of wreaking tremendous physical havoc to personal property. Bulls that have escaped confinement are potentially dangerous because of their playful and unpredictable moods and may inadvertently injure themselves as they revel in freedom from the restrictive restraints of fence and gate.

Racing to the house, I raised the alarm. Having grown accustomed to such middle-of-the-night emergencies, I was soon joined outside by my seventeen-year-old son Clay, my twelve-year-old son Jace, and my wife Laraine—who is twenty-nine years of age (and has been for as long as I can remember, and will be for as long as I know what's good for me). Laraine and Jace took up defensive positions along the perimeter of our feedlot in order to protect our neighbors from any rampaging bulls. Clay, with bullwhip in hand and dog at side, began to gather the scattered animals. I ran ahead to determine who had escaped and how.

As I came to pen seven, my flashlight revealed the gate wide open and that all fifteen of our oldest and most mature bulls were on the loose. As these facts registered cognitively, my mind unpredictably skipped to Jesus' parable of the lost sheep. The image of a solitary lamb straying from the safety of the fold stayed with me as we frenetically searched for the missing bulls in the darkness of the dust-filled air. Finally, after waking all the neighbors with our excited hoopla, we closed the gate on the last escapee. All strays were accounted for and returned safely to the fold.

In our tempestuous world of great uncertainty and danger, the only safe fold we have as mortals is within the covenant boundaries of the gospel of Jesus Christ. That truth is never fully comprehended by the secular world, and because the fences and gates that enclose mankind are all self-made and voluntarily restrictive, we wander aimlessly along the alleys of mortality, carelessly destroying the lines connecting us to the waters springing up unto everlasting life. Following God's prescribed plan of salvation is the only security in an insecure world, and learning that it is like finding a glittering vein of gold in a mountain of pyrite. Discovering this treasured truth is a priceless endowment to the spiritually-minded man of Christ, but it is foolishness to the natural man and the carnally-minded.

Commenting on the value of following His plan, the Savior said:

"And, if ye keep my commandments and endure to the end, ye shall have eternal life which gift is the greatest of all the gifts of God" (D&C 14:7).

Elsewhere he expands that truth with this doctrine:

"But learn that he who doeth the works of right-eousness shall receive his reward, even peace in this world, and eternal life in the world to come" (D&C 59:23).

If eternal life is the greatest gift or blessing God can bestow upon us as immortals, then certainly its nearest mortal equivalent is peace in this world. But where in this world of strife and conflict can peace be found?

Chuck Miller, a friend of mine, fought in many of the amphibious assaults in the Pacific in the last year and a half of World War II. On one island the Marines had made a successful beach landing and were employing a pincer strategy to squeeze the enemy into an untenable position in the middle of the island. Chuck and four other men were selected to go on a scouting mission to determine the exact location of Japanese forces.

Each member of the scouting squadron was assigned a specific travel corridor; one man in front, one man on each side, one man in the rear, and the squad leader in the middle. This diamond formation allowed them mobility as a unit because they could communicate with each other by using prearranged signals on a steel comb. A strum with the fingers along the teeth of the comb sounded like a cricket and harmonized with the jungle's nocturnal noises. One strum meant stop, two meant proceed, three sharp strums meant get down, and four meant come together in the middle.

On this night, Chuck was on the right wing and moving cautiously forward. The night was pitch black and the air humid because of the density of the overhanging foliage. The jungle was alive with the sounds of insects and birds, and the movement of snakes and wild animals. Despite being only yards away from the other members of the scout team, they were invisible to him. As Chuck strained his senses to perceive what was around him, he heard the three-strum signal and immediately dropped to the jungle floor.

As he lay hidden underneath the protective canopy of a tree, he heard the tramp of boots and knew that the jungle around him was filled with enemy soldiers on the move. He silently waited for them to pass. His heart began to pound wildly within his chest. Filled with terror, he willed himself into immobility as a contingent of enemy soldiers passed within inches of his hiding place. The last Japanese soldier came abreast of Chuck and inexplicably stopped. The soldier was standing in such close proximity that the tip of his boot was against Chuck's leg. Fearful that his breathing might reveal his vulnerable position, Chuck refrained from expulsing air. The intense emotional pressure caused capillaries in his nose and ears to burst. With blood streaming down his face he waited for his fate to be decided. After what seemed an eternity, the enemy soldier finally moved on.

In this world where wars and rumors of wars are a prophesied fact of life, peace must be more than merely the absence of conflict and must be present even in terrifying circumstances. For those who trust in Christ and in his plan of happiness, peace is a comforting reality. Jesus said:

"Peace I leave with you, my peace I give unto you: not as the world giveth, give I unto you. Let not your heart be troubled, neither let it be afraid" (John 14:27).

Jesus, in his role as a mortal Messiah, was called the Prince of Peace, and that it is he who speaks peace to our minds and souls in times of difficulty and distress. Peace is the opposite of fear, and its receipt is predicated upon our personal righteousness and the degree of faith we have cultivated in our Savior. The blessing of peace, like the gift of eternal life, while always available to us is not gratuitously granted. Both peace and eternal life come only to those who repent and sanctify themselves before the Lord. For example, the Nephites, under King Benjamin's monarchy, were filled with joy and peace of conscience after they were sanctified by the Holy Ghost and received a remission of their sins.

To sanctify is to make holy or sacred. Sanctification is the process of personal purification which we initiate through yielding our hearts unto God, and which is culminated by the purifying presence of the Holy Ghost. As we do yield our hearts unto God, we become meek and willing to do whatever the Lord requires of us in order to receive the fellowship of the Holy Spirit. His requirements to us are simple and clear.

"Let thy bowels also be full of charity towards all men, and to the household of faith, and let virtue garnish they thoughts unceasingly; then shall thy confidence wax strong in the presence of God; and the doctrine of the priesthood shall distil upon thy soul as the dews from heaven.

"The Holy Ghost shall be thy constant companion, and thy scepter an unchanging scepter of righteousness and truth;. . ." (D&C 121:45-46).

To receive the sanctifying companionship of the Holy Ghost requires us to be filled with charity and virtue. Charity is that same pure love that emanated from Christ, a love freely given without expectation of reciprocity or reward. It is a love bestowed on the true followers of Jesus Christ and is a distinguishing characteristic of his disciples.

One morning, while on their mission in Vermont in the early 1960s, my grandparents arose to go proselytizing. As was their habit before leaving, they knelt in prayer to ask the Lord for direction. At the conclusion of the prayer Grandpa turned to Grandma and said, "Mother, we will not go proselyting today." When she inquired why, he replied the Lord had something else in mind for them and would direct their activities. She meekly accepted his reply and together they set off on this undefined assignment.

In the little village of Cobblestone, just before Waterbury, they felt impressed to stop and call upon an elderly widow. They knocked on her door, but received no reply. Not satisfied, they climbed the stairs to the tenants who rented an upstairs apartment from her, and asked them whether they had seen Sister Farnum. "No, not for two days," came the reply. Grandpa asked whether there was another way into her house. Yes, there was a stairway down the back of their apartment.

Grandma and Grandpa descended the stairs into her home. It was dark and quiet. They found a light switch and turned it on. "Oh, my goodness, she's dead," Grandpa exclaimed, as he rushed to an inert body on a cot in the back of the room. He grasped her wrist and felt a faint pulse. Immediately he administered to her through the power of the priesthood. As he closed the blessing her eyes flickered open and she grabbed his hand.

Grandpa asked what was wrong and if there was anything they could do for her. She mutely pointed to the refrigerator. Grandma went to it and opened it. The lone content of the fridge was a small carton of milk. They took the milk and helped Sister Farnum swallow a sip. In a few minutes they gave her more milk and color began to return to her cheeks. At last, when she could talk, she reported that she had been lying immobile on the cot for two days, too weak to move, unable to call for help, and only able to pray. Before leaving her they arranged for food, medical assistance, and a caregiver to look after her.

Jesus said:

> "For I was an hungered, and ye gave me meat: I was thirsty, and ye gave me drink: I was a stranger and ye took me in:
> "Naked, and ye clothed me: I was sick, and ye visited me: I was in prison, and ye came unto me" (Matthew 25:35-36).

> ". . . Inasmuch as ye have done it unto one of the least of these my brethren, ye have done it unto me" (Matthew 25:40).

Christ's charity towards us extends even beyond the boundaries of grave and death, but to be realized by his mortal children, it must be manifested by his living servants. Charity, like faith, becomes reality only as we express it in our good works towards others.

Virtue is that quality of moral excellence and probity that is the very nucleus of Christ's character. Virtue is akin to holiness and implies purity of thought and action. As members of the Church we profess a belief in seeking after that which is virtuous. The prophet Isaiah informs us that God's thoughts and actions are higher than man's thoughts and actions (Isaiah 55:8-9). Seeking for this path of virtue places us on the high road to perfection. The more virtuous we become, the closer our thoughts and ways rise to Christ's level of mental cerebration and decisive action.

In 1838 at Far West, Missouri, William W. Phelps was dropped from the Presidency of the Church in Missouri by action of the High Council. Instead of acknowledging his transgression and repenting, he turned against the Church and especially against Joseph Smith. He became instrumental in betraying the leaders of the Church to the Missouri militia, and later testified in court against them. As a result of his actions, the prophet Joseph was incarcerated in the ironically-named Liberty jail. The other faithful members of the church suffered unspeakable hardship and privation as they were driven out of Missouri at gunpoint.

After experiencing bitter remorse of conscience, two years later William W. Phelps wrote Joseph Smith a letter expressing his excruciating sorrow and regret, and pleaded for readmission into the church. Despite all that he had suffered, despite all the saints had suffered, Joseph Smith eschewed vindictiveness and answered in a Christlike, virtuous manner. Here are excerpts from his response to William W. Phelps:

Dear Brother Phelps:

I must say that it is with no ordinary feelings I endeavor to write a few lines to you . . .

You may in some measure realize what my feelings, as well as Elder Rigdon's and Brother Hyrum's were, when we read your letter. Truly our hearts were melted into tenderness and compassion when we ascertained your resolves. I can assure you I feel a disposition to act on your case in a manner that will meet the approbation of Jehovah (whose servant I am), and agreeable to the principles of truth and righteousness which have been revealed . . .

It is true, that we have suffered much in consequence of your behavior. The cup of gall, already full enough for mortals to drink, was indeed filled to overflowing when you turned against us. One with whom we had oft taken sweet counsel together, and enjoyed many refreshing seasons from the Lord. Had it been an enemy, we could have borne it . . .

However, the cup has been drunk, the will of our Father has been done, and we are yet alive, for which we thank the Lord. And having been delivered from the hands of wicked men by the mercy of our God, we say it is your privilege to be delivered from the powers of the adversary . . .

Believing your confession to be real, and your repentance genuine, I shall be happy once again to give you the right hand of fellowship, and rejoice over the returning prodigal.

Come on, dear brother, since the war is past,

For friends at first, are friends again at last.

Yours as ever, Joseph Smith Jun.

Regardless of our position in life, all of us are prodigals trying to find our way safely back to our Heavenly Father's fold. Our only mortal assurance of our eventual immortal destiny lies in that sublime feeling of peace that comes to us as we exercise our agency in seeking after that which is virtuous and charitable. As we sanctify ourselves by yielding our hearts and minds to God, the day will come when we shall see Him, and shall stand in his presence comfortably, confidently, knowing that we legitimately belong there because we have become like him in thought and deed.

Chapter 4

Gospel Signals

It was a bright, fresh Saturday morning in mid-March. The air was fragrant with the smell of sage, but the breeze that blew carried a cool edge to it. The horses could smell the wild, free aromas of the brush and snorted nervously as we unloaded them from our trailer. My seventeen-year-old son, Clay, had brought along a two-year-old colt that had not been ridden anywhere except in the confines of our own pens at home. The strangeness of this new environment made the inexperienced colt fidget and paw the dirt as he was led around in preparation to riding. As Clay swung his leg over the saddle, the colt responded by exploding high into the air: once, twice, thrice. Oblivious to the constraining hackamore pulling against his nose, the acrobatic young horse continued to jump—seven, eight, nine times before finally yielding to the pressure on him to stop.

After that adrenaline-stirring beginning, my two sons and I trotted our horses up the trail. Clay's colt continued to act skittish so he determined to take the starch out of him by riding straight over the top of a steep hill. My other son and I maintained our position on the trail with the understanding that we would meet him on the other side. After a brisk ride around the base of the hill and then up the inclining path on the far side, we arrived at the rendezvous point. Clay was not there.

As we waited for him, a sense of uneasiness descended upon me. My anxiety was confirmed when we heard the muffled report of three pistol shots fired in rapid succession echoing on the side of the hill we had just left. Recognizing the shots as a signal for help, but having no firearm to send a responding message that we were coming, we turned our horses around and rushed to his aid. Since he had no way of knowing that help was on its way, he continued to fire his pistol as a distress signal.

As we came around the final turn in the trail, Clay came into view. He walked towards us with a grimace on his countenance and his chin smeared with brown mud. His horse was not in sight. According to his story, he had almost made it to the mountain crest when the colt whirled around and began to buck sideways down the hill. Worried that the awkward angle of his descent would topple the colt on top of him, he yanked the horse's head around so that now he was pointed straight down. As the two of them rocketed down the steep slope, the colt suddenly ducked his head, planted his front legs stiffly into the dirt, and came to a screeching halt. Clay sailed over the horse's head and skied down the hillside face first until his chin had built up sufficient friction in the dirt to act as a brake. In retrospect, he commented that it was a good thing that the horse ran off; otherwise he would have been sorely tempted to aim his signal shots in its direction.

In a world glutted with perplexing and contradictory choices, there are so very many of God's children who find it difficult to discern between the false and the genuine. For them, mortality sometimes resembles a turbulent gallop over the top of a steep mountain rather than a peaceful ride on a well-maintained trail. Frustrated by the wild course of their lives, those who desire to find a better way send out distress signals with the hope that someone will hear and respond to their cry for help.

Regardless of how faint or how loud the signal, distress cries are always heard. Satan and his minions are keenly attuned to the sound of struggling mortals attempting to escape their devilish traps. Like predatory coyotes on the prowl, calls of distress always draw them in for the kill.

Fortunately, that God who can account for the life of a solitary sparrow also hears the faintest whimper from his mortal children. As President Spencer W. Kimball observed:

"God does notice us, and he watches over us. But it is usually through another person that he meets our needs. Therefore, it is vital that we serve each other."

If we, as consecrated members of the church, do not respond to signals for help from our struggling brothers and sisters then we have failed in our most fundamental covenant responsibility. Failing to respond to cries for aid in times of spiritual distress is tantamount to signing spiritual death certificates. If we do not arrive with a compass and first aid when direction and healing are required, we can be certain that Satan and his ravenous pack of coyotes will not be so negligent, and will soon smother all plaintive cries for help.

What then can we do to fulfill our covenant responsibility to bear one another's burdens and comfort those who stand in need of comfort? First, we need to be skilled at recognizing signals for help. Second, we need to respond by sending clear signals that help is available. Third, we need to signal which of life's trails lead to spiritual safety. With different emphasis we need charity, hope, and faith.

Many years ago, while working as a herdsman on a large dairy in Minersville, Utah, it was my duty to hire the milkers. On one occasion I was approached by two Navajo boys who had come up from the reservation in Arizona. The boys were cousins, both sixteen years old, and full of smiles and good humor. I was impressed with their willingness to work and hired them. They turned out to be good milkers, were simple and unpretentious, and were pleasant to be around.

During that same period one of our other milkers was an unpleasant man by the name of Walter. Walter had a dour, suspicious outlook on life. He was mean-spirited and was forever fomenting trouble with the other employees. He had worked at several dairies, and although he was an excellent milker, had been forced to leave each job because of his belligerent attitude. He publicized the fact that he carried around a loaded pistol, and that he wouldn't hesitate to use it if his fists didn't carry enough weight. Walter was a bully, and most of the people around the dairy were cowed by his presence and thus steered clear of him.

For whatever reason, Walter carried a grudge against the two Navajo boys. Soon reports circulated to me that he was threatening them whenever they worked the evening shift together. One night around midnight, I awoke to a frantic knocking on my front door. Rubbing sleep from my eyes, I cautiously opened the door and discovered the two young Lamanites shivering and shaking on my porch. I invited them into my house, where they related a bizarre tale of Walter pursuing them all over town with his pistol. They were terrified, and since they had no family or friends in the community to protect them, they signaled for my help. I assuaged their fears, calmed them down, and assured them that I would enlist the protective aid of local law authorities. The next morning, before I could enact my promise, the boys quietly slipped out of town and hitchhiked back to the reservation where they could be insulated against evil in an environment of caring concern and love.

In the concluding chapters of the Book of Mormon, the prophet Mormon gives us a lesson on charity. From him we learn that charity is a gift bestowed only upon the true followers of Jesus Christ, and that it is defined as a pure, everlasting, and perfect love. The most obvious fruits of charity possession are the Christlike characteristics of patience, kindness, humility, temperance, faith, and faithfulness.

Because charity is a Godlike love, it awakens in us a divinely-centered awareness and perception of our fellowman. Our eyes may then become single to the glory of God, and when that happens our bodies and minds will become sanctified from darkness and evil, so that we comprehend all things. Because of the quickening of our spiritual senses through charity, we hear, see, and recognize the subtle distress signals sent out by our fellowman. Charity compels us to respond to those signals as Christ would respond; calming fears, comforting hearts, binding wounds, and showing the way. Charity is the divine language of love—a language that we must become fluent in if we are to effectively aid our spiritually-groping brothers and sisters.

My great-great grandmother Bushnell came across the plains with the pioneers when she was just a small girl. One morning after leaving Winter Quarters, her mother got down from the wagon seat and placed in her arms her infant sister. Her mother instructed her to ride in the wagon with the baby while she walked behind and picked berries. When the noon hour arrived and the wagon train stopped for lunch, her mother was nowhere in sight. A worried group of men back-tracked to the spring they had left that morning. Although they carefully searched the ground on both sides of the trail, they were unable to find any trace of her.

With the pervasively sinister influence of Satan in these latter days, it is increasingly common for good people to be lost on the trail leading to eternal life. These decent people become so confused and befuddled by the many alternate paths beckoning to them that they lose sight of orienting landmarks. Without landmarks to guide them through mortality, they wander in hopeless circles, ever learning, but never able to come to a knowledge of the truth. At some point they recognize the emptiness and futility of their journey, and despair of ever realizing any of the deeper emotions such as joy and peace. As life grows increasingly superficial, they grow increasingly despondent.

Years ago, on a hunting trip in the Chiricahua mountains of southern Arizona, one of our companions became lost. As night descended, my father and I built a huge bonfire on the top of a hill with the hope that in the darkness of the night our lost companion would see our signal of light and orient himself to the direction of camp.

Our signal, to the lost souls of the world, is to hold up the light that is in Christ. He is the light that shineth in darkness. Through him the despair which comes from following the misguided paths of the world can be erased and replaced with hope. One of the fundamental doctrines of the gospel of salvation is that hope comes through the atoning sacrifice of Jesus Christ. Our responsibility, then, to those individuals signaling for help is to hold up the effulgent light of Christ as a responding signal that hope is available, that it will come to all who earnestly seek it, and that it is found in the doctrine of Christ's atonement.

While attending a Race Relations class at Boise State University, Sister Kathy Hoppell of Emmett, Idaho, found herself thinking of other things. Although her elderly sociology professor was an affable man, she did not find him exceptionally interesting. On this particular day she was sitting in the back of the room, and as a middle-aged white woman, was a distinct minority in this class of sixty students.

Suddenly her attention was ratcheted back to her professor as his voice deepened and volume increased and she heard him say in a booming voice, "When my uncle was a young father struggling to make a living, his Mormon bishop came to his farm and asked him to pay his tithing. My uncle replied that he didn't have any money to pay tithing. The bishop requested that he give the church one of his horses for tithing. My uncle explained to the bishop that he had recently sold most of his horses to pay his bills and had only retained his favorite saddle horse as a means of transportation. The bishop marched to the barn, haltered the horse, and rode away with him. Neither my uncle or his family ever attended a Mormon church again."

While the professor lectured, he paced in front of the class in an agitated manner. His countenance and voice betrayed a deep-seated resentment, which the recitation of this story had evoked. Sister Hoppell listened with pounding heart, feeling that she must reply, but frightened that her emotions would sabotage her response. Silently she prayed for help.

In the momentary interlude following the conclusion of his story, Sister Hoppell spoke up in a loud, steady voice saying, "Brother, there is no bishop in the Mormon church that would have taken your uncle's horse for tithing. The Mormon church did not need your uncle's horse or his money."

The professor stopped his pacing and stood in front of the class in incredulous silence. For long moments he stood speechlessly mute, staring at Sister Hoppell, perhaps stunned at being addressed by the honorific title of Brother. Finally he said, "I think you're right. I think my uncle gave the bishop the horse and then blew the story out of proportion."

In the babel of misdirecting voices in the world, our voices, as members of the true church of Jesus Christ must be clear and certain. As the Apostle Paul put it:

> "For if the trumpet give an uncertain sound, who shall prepare himself to the battle?
> "So likewise ye, except ye utter by the tongue words easy to be understood, how shall it be known what is spoken?. . ." (1 Cor. 14:8-9).

We have been commissioned as emissaries of Jesus Christ

to proclaim his gospel of salvation. It is only through our faith in Christ that we are able to open our mouths in awkward, frightening situations, and with certitude verbally signal the correct path to eternal life.

Even when our message is articulated clearly and transmitted through the instrumentality of the Holy Ghost, empirical experience tells us that the response to our signal of truth will vary. There will be those who will not recognize any truth. Others will recognize it, but because of the cares of the world will reject it. Still others will recognize the truth, rejoice in finding it, but not have sufficient faith to carry them any distance on the path leading to eternal life. Finally there are the pure in heart, who patiently seek for a directional signal from heaven, who recognize it when it comes, who embrace the truth, and who then awaken to a vibrant, energetic faith in Christ.

Jesus Christ is the way, the truth, and the light of the world. As his mortal servants it is our duty to point the way, express the truth, and light the path for those who are spiritually distressed both in and out of the church. As we act towards our fellowman with faith, hope, and charity we are promised a forgiveness of our sins (D&C 84:61), and everlasting joy in company with those to whom we helped signal the gospel's saving light (D&C 18:13-16).

Chapter 5

Spiritual Harmony

*"To every thing there is a season, and a time to
every purpose under the heaven;*

*"A time to be born, and a time to die; a time to
plant, and a time to pluck up that which is planted;*

*"A time to kill, and a time to heal; a time to break
down, and a time to build up;*

*"A time to weep, and a time to laugh; a time to
mourn, and a time to dance;*

*"A time to cast away stones, and a time to gather
stones together; a time to embrace, and a time to
refrain from embracing;*

*"A time to get, and a time to lose; a time to keep,
and a time to cast away;*

*"A time to rend, and a time to sew; a time to keep
silence, and a time to speak;*

*"A time to love, and a time to hate; a time of war,
and a time of peace"* (Ecclesiastes 3:1-8).

I remember our situation a few years ago during a time of
poverty. One day my son Clay was telling me all of the things
we needed to buy around our place. I listened patiently,
agreeing that it was a reasonable and desirable list, but then
launched into a parental sermon on how tight our money
supply was. For my coup d' grace, I explained that the federal
tax deadline was looming around the corner and things were so
bad I might have to sell Dakota, my favorite saddle horse, to

pay the tax bill. Clay gasped in astonishment, knowing how much I valued the horse, and how much he loved him, too.

As he pondered our difficult financial state a quizzical expression came over his face and he asked, "Dad, what would happen if we just kept Dakota and you didn't pay your taxes?"

"I would go to jail," I replied.

He looked earnestly at me and said, "Well, in that case, when do you think you'll get out?"

Because the nature of mortality is progression through opposition, life brims with choices; not all of them as clear-cut as deciding between horses and dads, taxes or jail. Lehi, in his last mortal sermon, divided agency into two opposing camps.

> *"Wherefore, men are free according to the flesh; and all things are given them which are expedient unto man. And they are free to choose liberty and eternal life, through the great Mediator of all men, or to choose captivity and death, according to the captivity and power of the devil; for he seeketh that all men might be miserable like unto himself"* (2 Ne. 2:27).

We, as covenant members of the church, are consciously trying to be doers of the word, actively choosing liberty and eternal life. As we immerse ourselves in the demands of being a disciple of Christ, we discover that our choices are not limited to the simple expedient of good over evil, but rather the more complex and agonizing choice between good and better.

As we obediently pursue the path to infinite perfection, we discover that we are handicapped by the finite properties of time and energy. Failure to comprehend these limitations leads to a type of spiritual neurosis characterized by frenetically running after whatever sin of omission we currently feel guilty about. Like the dog chasing his own tail, we go round and round, busily moving, but going nowhere. Circular and not upward spiritual motion leads to frustration, unhappiness, and despair.

Ataraxia is a word coined by the ancient Greeks meaning *peace of mind and emotional tranquility.* Of all the diverse populations on earth, we as Latter-day Saints should be the most ataractic. My observations as a priesthood leader indicate that many of us are not, and that the reason we are not is (ironically) our obsession with perfection. Intellectually we may acknowledge that perfection is a process, but emotionally we cling to the belief that it is a singular event and we want it to happen right now.

When we find ourselves in this state of anxiety we frequently turn to reflective analysis to determine what is wrong. Because we labor under a heavy burden of expectations, our diagnosis usually renders a verdict that somehow we are unbalanced in our daily efforts. Our self-prescribed antidote is to work even harder to bring that elusive and mysterious quality of balance back into our lives. Unfortunately, our diagnostic tools are tainted by our worldly perspective, which elevates work but discounts faith.

As a consulting dairy nutritionist and livestock manager, I know a few things about balance. For the last twenty years dairies have hired me to balance their rations for their milk cows. To balance a ration means that I formulate a diet that matches nutrient requirements with productive objectives and maintenance needs. What they don't know is that there are literally dozens of ways that I can balance their ration to match theoretical requirements. But theories sometimes do not harmonize with actual experience, and must be tuned to a more pragmatic pitch.

A skilled nutritionist sifts through the management details available to him and prioritizes his decisions according to what he rationalizes as most important. For example, in addition to listening to the herdsman who manages the cows, and the feed man who feeds the cows, I try to listen to the cows themselves. The language of the bovine is body language. As I carefully observe them in their own environment they communicate a great deal to me. As I walk amongst the cows I ask them certain questions, which they answer in their own inimitable way. Are you thin or are you fat? Are you ruminating or are you dyspeptic? Are you comfortable or are you stressed? Are you healthy or are you diseased?

From these and other facts, I deduce the type of feeds I should employ, and the types of supplements I need to incorporate. Generally I also recommend changes in their feeding and management practices to enhance the improved diet. What I ultimately seek for as a professional is not a simple balancing of nutritional needs, but rather a harmonious confluence of management practices and physical requirements. If everything is in harmony, the cows are much more productive and are noticeably healthier.

Likewise it is the harmonious blend of faith and works that we should strive for in our pursuit of perfection. Spiritual harmony is realized as we concentrate our energies on the prevailing task, taking care of the things we can control, and after having put forth our best effort, taking comfort in our faith that Heavenly Father will satisfy the remaining requirements and that our offering is acceptable unto Him.

Joseph Smith said:

> "Therefore, dearly beloved brethren, let us cheerfully do all things that lie in our power; and then may we stand still, with the utmost assurance, to see the salvation of God, and for his arm to be revealed" (D&C 123:17).

Brigham Young said:

> "To make ourselves happy is incorporated in the great design of man's existence. I have learned not to

*fret myself about that which I cannot help. If I can do
good, I will do it; and if I cannot reach a thing, I will
content myself to be without it. This makes me happy
all the day long."*

King Benjamin said:

*"And see that all these things are done in wisdom
and order; for it is not requisite that a man should run
faster than he has strength. And again, it is expedient
that he should be diligent, that thereby he might win
the prize; therefore, all things must be done in order"*
(Mosiah 4:27).

There is an orderly progression to life, and a time for every
purpose. Between the ages of nineteen and twenty-one I was a
dedicated full-time missionary. In my stage of life now I don't
have as much time for missionary work, and most of my energy
is expended in providing for my family spiritually and tempo-
rally. So it goes for each phase of our lives. Roles change,
priorities shift, but time marches on. And while we do not
neglect our responsibilities and obligations, still we should take
them in stride, faithfully performing our duty at the proper
time, satisfied with steady if unspectacular progress towards
perfection.

Edward Everett Hale is credited with saying:

"I am only one, but still I am one.

I cannot do everything, but still I can do something;

And because I cannot do everything

I will not refuse to do the something that I can do."

In the winter of 1992, an abundance of snow hit our area of
southwest Idaho. Sawyer's Pond behind our house was frozen
over and covered with powdery snow. One afternoon my kids
and I crossed over to the lake and slid down the side banks
directly onto the flat, frozen surface of the water. For the next
hour we played on the ice. When we had finished with our fun,

we were red-nosed from the biting cold and red-cheeked from our exertions.

Our return home required that we descend a steep hill and cross a plank bridge, which spanned the stream dividing our property from the lake. Because of the deep snow on the ground, the climb down to the bridge was slick and treacherous. To accommodate our safe passage, I stayed at the top and held a long rope which the kids grasped as they backed slowly down the slope. When they had all descended and crossed safely, I straddled our inner tube and prepared to slide down the hill, confident that I would come to a stop on the bridge.

My ride down was exhilarating and rapid, but when I came to the bridge I discovered my calculations were slightly askew. Instead of gliding smoothly onto the wooden plank spanning the stream, I smashed into its raised edge, which caused my inner tube to come to an abrupt halt. I, however, did not. As if in slow motion, I saw the startled looks on the faces of my kids as I flew over the bridge and crash-landed with a drenching plop in the water below. Instead of well-deserved sympathy or even concern for my welfare, my icy immersion in the stream generated an outburst of laughter from my children, who found my predicament more hilarious than life-threatening.

So often in life, we find ourselves so exhilarated by the speed we are traveling that we sometimes miss a bridge that we need to cross. There are many such bridge connections on the road to eternal life, and wisdom dictates that we travel at a speed harmonious to safe crossing. As we journey through life, we must remember that there is a time and a season for each of God's purposes for us. As we harmonize faith and works, we will witness the perfecting power of Jesus Christ in fulfillment of those purposes.

Chapter 6

Hold the High Ground

To the west of the small Pennsylvania town of Gettysburg is a series of ridges, and to the south stand two prominent hills. On one of those prominent points known as Cemetery Hill, General John Buford of the Union Army surveyed the land below him and the Confederate infantry, which was camped just outside this peaceful farming community.

Buford had two brigades of cavalry under his command, an armed force of 2500. He had been scouting the movements of the Rebel armies for five days, watching and wondering where they would strike next in their invasion of the north. It appeared that their armies were gathering here, and since he also knew that the Union armies were marching this direction, he inferred that the intersecting collision would take place at Gettysburg.

Buford was a shrewd and experienced military man. Knowing the likelihood of battle, he clearly saw the strategic advantage that would be gained by occupying the heights above the town. In his mind, the battle would be won by whoever held the high ground.

But now General Buford faced a serious dilemma: The nearest Union army under General John Reynolds was a full day's march away. A large Confederate deployment led by A.P. Hill was already camped at Seminary Ridge to the west. General Robert E. Lee was a tactical genius and upon arrival would immediately perceive the advantage of the high ground to the south of Gettysburg. Buford was terribly outnumbered.

He could justifiably retreat to the safety of his own army but sensed that unless he held these hills for the advancing Federal forces, the Union would face yet another ignominious defeat, a defeat that likely would spell doom for any hope of a reconciled United States of America.

That evening, June 30, 1863, he ordered his men to dismount and dig into the side of the ridges. His uncluttered strategy was to hold the high ground as long as possible. If they could hold out long enough, General Reynolds and his troops would come to their relief from the east.

The morning of July 1st dawned with low clouds and misty rain. An advance group of Rebel soldiers moved toward the hills on a scouting reconnaissance, not expecting resistance. They were surprised to be repulsed by steady fire from entrenched Union troopers. They backed up and organized an assault. Suddenly the piercing Rebel scream broke the mornings quiet and a full-scale charge hit the Union line. The scream soon choked off in agony as the cavalrymen, on higher ground and armed with seven shot carbine repeaters, unerringly picked off the advancing Rebel soldiers.

The Confederates again backed off and regrouped. Rolling their cannon into position they lobbed shells at the entrenched Union line. Under cover of their artillery they massed a division of 10,000 for a general assault. The Yankee cavalrymen hunkered down in their trenches, counted their rounds of ammunition, and grimly prepared to pour down death upon the soldiers coming up from below.

Once again a blood-curdling war cry interrupted the morning's quiet, and line upon line of young men and boys dressed in Rebel uniform surged bravely up the hill. Firing and advancing, they stormed the hilltop like an angry sea tossing wave after wave against a resistant shore. The Federal troops responded in unison, mowing down the Rebels with deadly fire from above. As Confederate casualties mounted, the soldiers doggedly fought on, stepping over the crumpled bodies of their fallen comrades as they sought to capture the high ground.

The fighting continued on and on in an interminable clash of wills, with sweat and blood and the anguished screams of the dying as backdrop for this horrific drama. When finally the Federal troopers could finger only a handful of rounds in their ammunition pouches, they knew their end was near. And then, miraculously, the attack ended as suddenly as it had begun. As the Confederates retreated hastily back down the hill, this small Federal force of Yankee cavalrymen raised a tired cheer. They had valiantly held the high ground against overwhelming odds.

But now their situation was appalling. General Buford knew that his exhausted and bloodied cavalry could not withstand another charge, and already Confederate reinforcements were massing at the bottom of the hill. When all hope was lost, when their sacrifice to preserve the high ground appeared to be for naught, General Buford turned hopefully to the east and, from the height of Cemetery Hill, saw his salvation. Line upon line of infantry troops dressed in Union blue were marching steadily towards his position. Help had arrived. Buford and his beleaguered cavalry had held the high ground. The Union was saved.

We live in a day of technological marvels. Because of the advanced sophistication of satellite transmission, ours is called the age of information. In this time of instantaneous global media coverage, reports of wars and rumors of wars circulate endlessly around us. Despite the news saturation of even the smallest of conflicts, there is one war that is overlooked and unreported. It may rightfully be called the war against ethical and moral standards, and it is a war that none of us can ignore because its battles are fought daily within the private chambers of our minds and hearts.

In our country today, starting at the highest levels of

government and industry, it appears that for many people the conflict to hold the high moral ground in the comportment of their individual lives is a losing battle. While the media gives no credence to the reality of this personal conflict, it does glamorize unethical, immoral, and antisocial behavior in the lives of its fictional characters and in its marketing icons. Ironically, after holding up such decadent behavior as an American ideal, its daily newscasts sensationalize reports of societal losses due to this same type of destructive, unethical and immoral behavior.

Admittedly, this is difficult and discouraging warfare, but because of the individual nature of the struggle there is always hope. Each day as we leave the security of home and family, and battle with the uncertainties of our professional environment, it is imperative to our individual self-worth that we conduct our affairs on a high level of personal integrity. To do this requires us to constantly compare the shifting ethical dynamics of the workplace with the immutable standards of righteousness set by the Savior.

Immersed in warfare from the time of his childhood, the prophet Mormon understood the ethical challenges inherent in an environment of relaxed moral strictures. Living in an era where good and evil were transposed in the public consciousness, he was able to remain uncorrupted in a period of almost universal immorality. Speaking to his fellow saints he gave this key instruction.

> "For behold, the Spirit of Christ is given to every man, that he may know good from evil; wherefore, I show unto you the way to judge; for every thing which inviteth to do good, and to persuade to believe in Christ, is sent forth by the power and gift of Christ; wherefore ye may know with a perfect knowledge it is of God.
>
> "But whatsoever thing persuadeth men to do evil,

and believe not in Christ, and deny him, and serve not
God, then ye may know with a perfect knowledge it is
of the devil; for after this manner doth the devil work,
for he persuadeth no man to do good, no, not one;
neither do his angels; neither do they who subject
themselves unto him" (Moroni 7:16-17).

On a frigid December night just before Christmas in 1975, I found myself walking the dark maternity pens of Shamrock Dairy in Tucson, Arizona. I was all alone, except for the presence of three hundred Holstein cows placidly waiting to give birth. I was there as a favor to my father, who as a professor in the Animal Science Department at the University of Arizona, was conducting an experiment on passive immunity in neonatal calves. All of his animal-physiology graduate students had abandoned him for the holidays, and he was left alone to finish an extensive piece of research work. Having just returned from a mission, I was available and willing.

As I made my rounds, I shone my flashlight on a cow lying on her side. She was rhythmically straining as though listening to some internal metronomic beat. I realized she would deliver a calf in just a few minutes and I turned back towards the office to collect my equipment. As I turned, a subliminal warning caused me to hesitate. I rotated back around and began to flash my light through the rest of the huge corral. The flashlight spotlighted the cows and bathed them in a surrealistic glow. Most were lying down peacefully chewing their cud, steam rising from their recumbent bodies. I skimmed the light into the most distant corner. There was something eerie and abnormal about that corner.

I began to walk toward it. For a few steps I thought my imagination was playing tricks on me. Then I saw it. Four red eyes momentarily flashed a reflection from my light. My heart increased its pumping rate, and every muscle and sense was on the alert as I forced myself to advance towards that far corner.

As I drew closer, my light revealed a grotesque tableau. Outlined in the flashlight's faint glow were two huge Doberman Pinscher dogs ravenously devouring the remains of a bacteria-ridden placenta.

The dogs did not move at my approach and welcomed me with ominous warning growls resonating deep within their throats. Although my arms and legs felt as though they had gelatinized, I bent down and armed myself with several large rocks. Mustering my courage, I emitted a shrill scream and rushed towards them while pelting them with rocks. The two Dobermans reluctantly gave ground, defiantly dragging the placenta with them as they retreated.

Tremulously I walked to the office, gathered my blood-collecting equipment, and then returned to the cow that had now calved. The calf was lying on the cold ground, vulnerable and helpless, wet, slimy and shivering. I pulled a blood sample from his neck, removed the calf from the cow before it could suckle, then began drying him with a fistful of straw. As the calf became more vigorous under my ministrations, I fed him a bottle of warm colostrum.

Colostrum is a mother's first milk, and in the case of this bull calf at Christmas time, the greatest gift his mother could bestow upon him. A calf is born without immunity to disease. Colostrum contains antibodies or immunoglobulins which the cow has built up in her own body and which are transferred to the calf when he drinks the colostrum. Colostrum would not protect the calf against the external threat of predatory dogs, but it would protect him against the more insidious threat of internal disease.

Like colostrum, integrity protects against the debilitating effects of internal turmoil when faced with external challenges. Integrity means moral soundness; it means conforming our actions and words to our personal ideals of excellence and truth. It means being true to correct principles formed from the matrix of gospel teachings and commandments.

Integrity's constituent antibodies include honesty, veracity, and honor. *Honesty* implies truthfulness, fairness in dealing, and absence of fraud, deceit and dissembling. *Veracity* is truthfulness of expression. *Honor* means strict adherence to our personal code of ethics and morality.

Without integrity to guide our decisions, we become vulnerable to the influence of human predators, who are rapaciously eager to supply us with conflicting choices, each choice bearing with it a specific consequence. Integrity's full immunizing and protective power is realized only in retrospect; when we have had time to reflect both on the blessings of proper conduct and the negative consequences of improper actions.

When I was eight years old, my parents gave me a Daisy air rifle for a Christmas present. Its velocity wasn't great, but I had an exhilarating time knocking over toy soldiers and living in the exciting world of my imagination. Along with the BB gun came strict covenants of conduct to which I willingly agreed. The paramount rule was that I was never to point my gun at another human being.

One day I was playing peacefully in my backyard, when a neighborhood boy, Bucky Bill, came over and perched on the cinderblock wall dividing our yard from the next. Bucky Bill was four years older than myself. He was tall and frail, and suffered from an obvious and embarrassing orthodontic problem. Because of the protrusion of his front teeth, he had received much unsolicited attention from other playmates, many of whom aptly compared him to a beaver. Bucky Bill, in turn, evened the scales of justice in life by tormenting those younger or weaker than himself. Since I qualified on both counts I had witnessed firsthand his talent at conjuring up insults.

On this particular day, Bucky Bill was at his infuriating best. I tried several retaliatory insults, but they appeared toothless and flat when compared to his sarcastic remarks. In desperation, I imagined for a minute the supreme satisfaction which could come from pulling him down from the wall and straightening out his teeth without the aid of Novocain. Having once attempted that, I recognized the futility of the action.

When at last I seemed doomed to endure his aspersions, a sudden inspiration flashed across my juvenile mind. I walked casually to the backdoor, opened it slightly, reached quietly inside and pulled out my trusty Daisy Red Rider. Hours of practicing on toy soldiers had honed my aim and reaction time. Before Bill could close his big mouth, I had cocked my rifle, aimed it, and sent a round copper BB speeding towards his chest. The bullet bounced off his T-shirt with a gratifying thud. Bucky Bill screamed in terror and toppled off the block wall.

For a few brief moments I gloried in my deed. I had finally conquered my nemesis, and that satisfying thought carried me back into the house where I intended to hide my weapon and my crime. Just as I entered my bedroom a softball-sized boulder crashed through the window, shattering the glass into a billion shards. As I stared in horror at the broken glass, an awful truth began to dawn on me: My actions could no longer be hidden from my parents. I had violated their trust and now would have to pay the consequences.

From that awakening experience and other similar ones, I learned that a man of integrity must always act in concert with his standards, must be incorruptible in the face of temptation, and must be scrupulous in fulfilling the trusts reposed in him by others. The Greek philosopher Aristotle wrote, "We are what we repeatedly do. Excellence, then, is not an act, but a habit." Remember—integrity is not an act, but a habit.

It was 1945. The night was black, and the waters of the Pacific Ocean were illuminated only by stars. My father was at the helm of a merchant marine ship, sailing to discharge a valuable cargo of fuel and supplies to U.S. Marines fighting in the Pacific theatre. The atmosphere on the ship was as tense as the night was dark. No running lights were allowed because this area of the Pacific was patrolled heavily by Japanese submarines.

While the ship's crew silently performed their duties or slept restlessly in their berths, the captain kept vigil high on the bridge. From his vantage point he carefully scanned the dark waters for any sign of obstacles, barking out directions as they became necessary. His instructions were forwarded by a first mate to my father who was steering the ship. All had been quiet for an extended period of time when suddenly the captain shouted to the first mate, "Starboard thirty degrees!" The first mate had succumbed to the rhythm of the waves against the ship and was dozing when the captain's orders had been issued. He awoke with a start and yelled "Port 30 degrees!"

My father had heard both commands. He was confused as to which course to follow. He had been rigorously trained to always obey the first mate's commands as his immediate superior. He also knew that the safety of the ship depended upon the captain. Finally, after an agonizing moment, he did as he had been trained to do and turned the ship thirty degrees to port. The captain, who had heard the first mate's erroneous order, rushed to the helm, took control of the wheel, and corrected the course of the ship.

Our lives are like ships sailing upon an ocean that is both dangerous and terrifying. For the most part we sail in hostile, shark-infested waters. Consequently, we must rely upon a steady hand to guide us through the high winds, the turbulent waves, the treacherous shoals and reefs that can so easily capsize and cripple our craft. The testing nature of mortality guarantees that no hand but ours will be at the wheel to steady the ship and keep it on course. Our only reliable compass in times of darkness and decision is that keen sense of personal integrity developed by focusing on the steady light of Christ, and confirmed by the affirmation of the Holy Ghost as we find the right way.

Chapter 7

The Worth of a Soul

When my son Clay was twelve years old and in the sixth grade, his body chemistry began to change and his underarms assumed an unpleasant aroma. Since his bathing habits had not kept pace with the development of his new body odor, there were times when the air in his vicinity was rather pungent. His two older sisters were particularly critical whenever they neared him, and insisted that he shower daily and use a strong underarm deodorant. After enduring criticism for a lengthy period of time, he finally capitulated and started showering every three days instead of every five. When his sisters berated him for not showering daily he argued that after he showered he applied two different kinds of stick deodorant to his underarms, and then followed that with Right Guard spray-on. Since each deodorant guaranteed protection for twenty-four hours he concluded he was adequately covered for three days.

We live in deceptive times; times when we absolutely need the guaranteed assurance of God's protective influence, without which we may be like the fully alive but inert body of King Lamoni, whom some said was dead and stinketh. In this age of deception it is important that we identify zones of safety and security. As we listen to the arguments of the two conflicting powers upon this earth, it becomes apparent that their intentions for our welfare are diametrically opposed.

"For behold, at that day shall he rage in the hearts of the children of men, and stir them up to anger against that which is good.

"And others will he pacify, and lull them away into carnal security, that they will say: All is well in Zion; yea, Zion prospereth, all is well—and thus the devil cheateth their souls, and leadeth them away carefully down to hell.

"And behold, others he flattereth away, and telleth them there is no hell; and he saith unto them: I am no devil, for there is none—and thus he whispereth in their ears, until he grasps them with his awful chains, from whence there is no deliverance.

"Yea, they are grasped with death, and hell; and death, and hell, and the devil, and all that have been seized therewith must stand before the throne of God, and be judged according to their works, from whence they must go into the place prepared for them, even a lake of fire and brimstone, which is endless torment" (2 Ne. 28:20-23).

Fortunately there is another power that persuades men without coercion or force.

"Remember the worth of souls is great in the sight of God;

"For, behold, the Lord your Redeemer suffered death in the flesh; wherefore he suffered the pain of all men, that all men might repent and come unto him.

"And he hath risen again from the dead, that he might bring all men unto him, on conditions of repentance.

"And how great is his joy in the soul that repenteth" (D&C 18:10-13).

During the scorching summer months of southern Arizona where I grew up, a swimming pool was the only cooling thing to be found in the parched Sonoran desert. In the summer of my eleventh year, my older brother fortuitously acquired a girlfriend who had one. As a strategy to obtain favor with my brother, she often invited us over to enjoy a swim.

While the romance was still going strong, my brother's girlfriend's identical twin nieces came down to spend some time with their grandparents. As fate would have it, they were my very own age. Being a normal eleven-year-old male, I was on the periphery of interest in females, and these two beautiful girls were swinging the pendulum toward a strong attraction. Although I soon fell in love with one of the girls, I wasn't sure which one it was. This was due to the fact that I couldn't tell them apart except by the different colors of their otherwise identical bathing suits. If they had been consistent about wearing the same-colored swimsuit for my visits, my problem would have been solved, my true love determined, and life would have been unmitigated bliss. However, they believed in the communal ownership of property, and from visit to visit I never knew which girl was in which bathing suit. Rather than risk censure and endanger my fragile relationship with the girls, I lived in a state of continual angst. I never dared ask them for the truth: who was who?

One of Satan's strategies, as explained by Nephi, is to confuse and befuddle by creating precepts of men that closely mimic and counterfeit the word of God. Frequently, good people reject gospel principles because they are only willing to give them a superficial glance, and are not willing to risk social censure by delving into the truth. To counteract this devilish ploy, the Lord instructs us to patiently, consistently extend charity to our neighbors and friends so that they can first feel the effects of gospel principles, and then see beyond the superficial to the substantive truth that guides our actions.

By contrast, sometimes we are guilty of judging others superficially, deciding arbitrarily whether they are gospel material. Through harsh experience we may learn that our eyesight is myopic, and that our opinion of our fellowman would be greatly enhanced if we viewed them under heaven's magnifying glass.

When I was a freshman at BYU, I received a phone call from a friend inviting me to accompany her on a field trip to the Utah State Mental Hospital with her upper division psychology class. As a favor to her, I reluctantly agreed to go.

Upon reaching the hospital, the psychology class met in a short orientation session where we were instructed to freely mingle with the patients, engaging them in conversation, and discovering their attitudes about life. Mingling and visiting with the elderly and children's wards was easy, but when we reached the adolescent ward I began to feel uncomfortable. The residents of this division were there for a wide variety of reasons, including wards of the state, runaways, drug addicts, and malefactors. Virtually all of them suffered from some form of emotional trauma.

Since I wasn't a member of the psychology class, and since many of these individuals were my own age, I was apprehensive about entering into conversation with them. I backed up against a wall and quietly observed the antics going on around me. As I watched, I couldn't help but reflect upon the profound differences between these social misfits and myself. These kids seemed foreign; they looked different, acted different, talked different, and even had their own peculiar aroma.

As I stood there musing upon these dissimilarities, I became aware of a handholding couple from the psychology class walking toward me down the hall. As they came abreast of me they stopped, flashed an ingratiating smile designed to win confidence, and then inquired of me what life was like living here. As I stammered incoherently for a reply, they emphatically nodded their heads and then moved on down the hall to the next resident.

Fortunately for you and me the Lord does not look on us as critically as we look on each other.

"...for the Lord seeth not as man seeth; for man looketh on the outward appearance, but the Lord looketh on the heart" (1 Sam. 16:7).

Every person who walks this earth has a mental image of himself engraven upon his mind's eye. This self-image or identity is developed through a person's environment and through their experiences, and is reflected in their outward personality. In our world, overemphasis on the physical appearance of an individual, and upon the symbols of fashion, opulence, and even goodness, gives a distorted self-image and a false view of the worth of a soul. This perspective is actively cultivated by the devil and his minions.

"They seek not the Lord to establish his righteousness, but every man walketh in his own way, and after the image of his own god, whose image is in the likeness of the world, and whose substance is that of an idol, which waxeth old and shall perish in Babylon, even Babylon the great, which shall fall" (D&C 1:16).

When I was in college I was an avid weightlifter. I took up lifting as a means of stress reduction, but soon found the adrenalin rush from pumping heavy weights was addictive. I gradually became obsessive about my workouts, even going to the extreme of taking weights with me to a family reunion. Eventually I came to realize that an obsession with lifting and bodybuilding, as with any habit, tends to distort our view of the world and especially of ourselves.

For a class assignment while in college, I composed a poem addressing the dichotomy of perspective between the outward beauty of the physical body and the inward shallowness of soul, which sometimes accompanies it.

He stands all tense like gods on Mt. Olympus stood.
His athletic frame once made Athens known;
And to poetic mind and fawning female's glance
His body, though unrobed and unadorned,
Is picturesque in its stance
And lionlike in its tone.
To one unleashed from maudlin, metaphoric verse he
    stands,
Naked and purple under blazing bulbs;
His eyes bulge frog-like with that vain, blank stare
That ponds and mirrors only can reflect,
And under whose hypnotic care
Muscles are powerless to protect.

As Latter-day Saints, our view of ourselves and our view of others is profoundly influenced by our understanding that we are the spiritual offspring of Heavenly parentage and are created in God's own image. Comprehending this truth protects us from the false and hypnotically-riveting images of the world in which we live.

Being created in God's image is more than simple physical resemblance. Potentially we have all of the spiritual DNA necessary to become a god like our Father who is in Heaven. Comprehension of the full import of our potential divinity requires three prerequisites:

First, we must acquire the character trait of *humility*. Humility is a recognition of our need for divine intervention in our lives, and comes to those who approach God with the prayer of faith. Those who humbly pray with a sincere desire for spiritual edification will be blessed with a knowledge of their personal weaknesses, along with the means to overcome them.

King Lamoni's father was mystified by the friendship of his son with the Nephite Ammon. Later, when Ammon's brother

Aaron visited his kingdom, he was willing to be instructed regarding the source of the bewildering change which had come over his son Lamoni. As Aaron taught him about God, the fall of Adam, Jesus Christ, the atonement, and the need for repentance, King Lamoni's father expressed his desire to receive the joy that comes from hope in Christ. His humility was so great that he was prepared to do anything required of him (including abdicating his monarchy) in exchange for the remission of his sins. As a consequence of his humility he experienced a transformation of mind and heart through the sanctifying influence of the Holy Ghost.

Second, we must be willing to act upon Christ's commandments even when we are uncertain or even doubtful of the end result. As we do his will, we learn the source of his promises and that we are capable of becoming like him.

Lonny Oleata was from California. He was 5'7" tall and weighed a muscular 170 pounds. His hair was thick and black and wavy, and he wore it long. His beard was heavy, full, and unkempt. He was a high school graduate, but college, like so much in his life, seemed irrelevant. He viewed his existence as a tangled maze of contradictions. At best it was merely confusing; at worst it was a galactic black hole where questions went in but no answers emerged. With Vietnam a threatening gleam on his horizon, with the dissolution of ethical principles amongst family and friends, Lonny decided to drop out of the mainstream of life. He bought a Harley and a leather jacket, and went in search of the answers to life's mysteries on the back roads of America.

Unknown, unloved, uncared for, he drifted aimlessly from town to town and state to state, unconcerned where life or his motorcycle took him. Still, he yearned for something or somebody to explain to him the purpose of his existence.

In the summer of 1971 he roared into a small Utah town. He had intended to drive through, but people were streaming in from all directions so he quieted his loud engine and went to investigate. On a hill at the north end of town was a large cathedral-type building. He had never seen anything quite like it. South of this building swirled a whirlpool of people and activity and so he plotted his course in that direction. Signs told him that this was the Mormon Miracle Pageant. He knew who the Mormons were, but he had never witnessed a miracle pageant before. His curiosity piqued, he found a place to sit down in the audience where he waited skeptically to see miracles performed.

Sitting next to him that night was a miracle in the form of a distinguished-looking middle-aged man. This kind man initiated a conversation with Lonny and found out the facts of his life. As scenes were enacted from the Book of Mormon, Lonny was impressed and began to ask questions. At the end of the evening the man next to him gave him a copy of the Book of Mormon with the instruction that if he would make the effort to read and pray about it, God would reveal the truth of it to him personally.

Lonny thumbed open the book. On its front page was a picture of a family and an inserted page declaring their belief in the truth of the contents of the book. As the man sitting next to him stood to depart, he handed Lonny a business card with the invitation to look him up at his office in Salt Lake City if he happened to come that direction.

Lonny was curious about the Book of Mormon but doubtful concerning its claims of truth. Skeptically at first, he began to read, and as he read he prayed. Having fulfilled the requirement to read and pray, he now received the promised blessing. A deep emotion welled within him and he felt the truth of the Book of Mormon. This experience was so unique in his life that he did not know what to do next.

Having no other plans, he hopped on his Harley and headed for Salt Lake City. He looked up the family who had donated the book and rang their doorbell. They invited him into their home. He stayed for several days. During that time he completed the Book of Mormon, visited Temple Square, and looked up the man who had sat next to him in Manti. His name was Vaughn Featherstone.

Lonny Oleata drove back to California. He was baptized there, and a few months later was called to serve in the Virginia Roanoke Mission where he completed a very successful, dedicated mission.

Third, we must have spiritually nurturing experiences with those more mature in the gospel than ourselves. It is these nurturing experiences in developing a personal perspective of who we are that are sometimes discounted as a means of acquiring celestial attributes.

The foundational basis for all that God does for us is *love*. He clearly wants us to reciprocate that love to our fellowman.

> *"We love him, because he first loved us.*
> *"If a man say, I love God, and hateth his brother, he is a liar: for he that loveth not his brother whom he hath seen, how can he love God whom he hath not seen?*
> *"And this commandment have we from him, That he who loveth God love his brother also"* (1 John 4:19-21).

In a gospel of love, each of us has been nurtured by others in times of spiritual need. To nurture means to nourish and feed. It also means to support and protect. One who nurtures is the equivalent of a mortal guardian angel, who guides callow spirits away from the dark, dour image of the world and toward the radiant countenance of Christ. To nurture another means that in times of trouble we are there with a comforting and kind word. It means that in times of temptation we are there with a cautionary admonition. It means that in times of trial we are there with a strong arm to lean on. And it also means that at those times of difficulty when we can't be there physically, our teachings and personality continue to exert a calming influence on the soul.

Listen to the experience of Enos, who was nurtured in his youth by his father Jacob:

> "Behold, it came to pass that I, Enos, knowing my father that he was a just man—for he taught me in his language, and also in the nurture and admonition of the Lord—and blessed be the name of my God for it—
>
> "And I will tell you of the wrestle which I had before God, before I received a remission of my sins.
>
> "Behold, I went to hunt beasts in the forests; and the words which I had often heard my father speak concerning eternal life, and the joy of the saints, sank deep into my heart.
>
> "And my soul hungered; and I kneeled down before my Maker, and I cried unto him in mighty prayer and supplication for mine own soul; . . ." (Enos 1:1-4).

Nurturing others by the good word of God may be the spark that ignites a soul to a lifetime of faithful allegiance to gospel principles. Contrarily, failing to spiritually nurture when the opportunity presents itself may have long-lasting ramifications on those individuals so neglected.

The Last Supper was painted by Leonardo Da Vinci, and the figures representing Christ and the Apostles were painted using living persons. The live model for the painting of the figure of Jesus was chosen first. When it was announced that Da Vinci would paint this picture, hundreds of young men were screened in an endeavor to find a face and personality exhibiting innocence and beauty, a face free from the dissipation of sin. After weeks of laborious searching, a virtuous young man of nineteen was selected. For six months Da Vinci painstakingly painted him as the living model of Christ.

During the next six years, other models were chosen to represent each of the eleven apostles. The last space on the canvas was reserved for Judas Iscariot. Once more Da Vinci went in search of the right model. For weeks he looked for a man with a countenance marked by deceit and hypocrisy; a face that delineated a character that would betray his best friend. Finally word filtered to the artist that a man whose appearance met his requirements had been found in a prison in Rome where he had been sentenced to die.

Da Vinci made the trip to Rome immediately. The prisoner was brought out of his dungeon. He was a swarthy man with long, unkempt hair, and a face scarred by viciousness and cruelty. Da Vinci had found his last model.

By special permission of the king, the prisoner was taken to Milan where the picture was being painted. For six months he sat daily in front of Da Vinci who transformed his likeness onto canvas. As he completed his last stroke, Da Vinci turned to the guards and instructed them to remove the prisoner. As the guards led the prisoner away he began to struggle with them, and with great exertion broke free of their grasp. The prisoner approached Da Vinci.

"Da Vinci," he cried in agitation, "Look at me! Do you not know who I am?"

Da Vinci scrutinized the man he had been painting for six months. "No, I have never seen you before you were brought before me out of the dungeon in Rome."

Lifting his eyes toward heaven the prisoner said, "O God, have I fallen so low?" Then turning his face to the painter he said, "Leonardo Da Vinci, look at me again, for I am the same man you painted just seven years ago as the figure of Christ."

Our lives are affected by the multiplicity of influences around us. In many instances it is those small, spiritually nurturing experiences bestowed upon us by Christlike men and women that turn out to be of real significance in our life. Their presence may be the lever that lifts us to the company and countenance of Jesus. Their absence may blight the soul and relegate us to the company and countenance of Judas. When we progress to that point in life where the worth of a soul becomes an important consideration in our behavior toward others, then we begin to comprehend our own divine potential.

Chapter 8

Self-reliance

While I was on my mission in Virginia, the Washington DC Temple was completed and dedicated. As the largest temple in the world, it is a very impressive structure. Erected on a hill amidst a small forest, its glistening white walls and spires rise above the surrounding trees. From the freeway below, the temple appears to be floating in air. That illusion is particularly heightened at night with the lights of the temple reflecting off the walls.

It was reported that one good southern Baptist gentleman thought that the end of the world was at hand when he was traveling on the Washington beltway for the first time late at night. He came around a bend in the freeway, and beheld an angelic being hovering above him in the air, holding a long trumpet, glowing with a golden light, and descending from on high. The car ended up in the ditch beside the freeway, the occupant still intact. It is presumed that our Baptist friend learned the difference between rapture and rupture.

Like our good brothers and sisters of other faiths, all of us are passengers in a vehicle traveling down a sinuous mortal highway. We do not know with certainty what is up ahead, around the corner, or to the sides. To be sure, there are road signs along the way; whether we perceive their true intent may ultimately determine our experiencing the difference between celestial rapture and telestial rupture.

In the beginning of our understanding, before the foundations of this world were laid, a great debate raged in the halls of our preexistent home. A blueprint for our eternal destiny had been proposed by our Father. This plan designated a Savior, an atonement, a resurrection, and a voluntary compliance to eternal law. It was a plan which entailed great risk on our part for it meant that we would walk by faith, not by sight, and that we would be responsible for our own actions and choices. The everlasting consequences of our obedience or disobedience would be acceptance into or banishment from the presence of our Father.

There were some who said that the risk was unacceptable and unnecessary. The leader of this dissident group was articulate in proposing an alternate plan that switched the burden of personal agency away from the individual, and placed it on a caretaker or overseer who would carefully manipulate the choices of his fellow mortals along a prescribed and monitored path.

This ideological debate gradually escalated from a flurry of heated words to a full-scale battle over the souls of men. Though the location of the engagement has shifted, that battle continues to this day. At the core of its contention is still the question of individual responsibility. On that topic President Spencer W. Kimball made this comment at the October 1977 General Conference.

"The responsibility for each person's social, emotional, spiritual, physical, or economic well-being rests first upon himself."

The principle of self-reliance is one of the distinguishing characteristics of Christ's gospel and a recurrent theme of emphasis within the church. In both modern and ancient times, the Savior and his prophets have taught repeatedly that the receipt of any blessing is contingent upon two things: individual faith and personal works.

For example, in a demonstration of parental concern, Alma instructs his two righteous sons, Helaman and Shiblon, that if they implicitly trust in God and obey his commandments they will be supported in their trials, troubles, and afflictions. Joseph Smith, in his lectures on faith, echoes a similar sentiment, stating that to have a rational, intelligent faith in God, men must believe that He exists and is a rewarder of those who do good.

The work portion of the equation involves the expenditure of mental, emotional, spiritual, and physical energy in actively seeking the Lord's blessings. The Lord instructs us that his blessings are predicated upon the faithful observance of specific commandments. But in addition, he teaches us this important doctrine:

> "For behold, it is not meet that I should command in all things; for he that is compelled in all things, the same is a slothful and not a wise servant; wherefore he receiveth no reward.
>
> "Verily I say, men should be anxiously engaged in a good cause, and do many things of their own free will, and bring to pass much righteousness;
>
> "For the power is in them, wherein they are agents unto themselves. And inasmuch as men do good they shall in nowise lose their reward" (D&C 58:26-28).

The Lord made Oliver Cowdery aware of this principle by informing him that his perfunctory act of prayer was not sufficient to solve the riddle of ancient scriptures. The lesson he apparently wished impressed upon Oliver's mind was that divine gifts were not gratuitously granted, but were realized only after he exercised his own powers of observation and thought.

Frank Hinton was a good friend of mine, a very practical man, and a repositor of great wisdom. One day our conversation turned to cattle, and he related an experience he had many years earlier. It seems that while Frank was living in Oregon, he had a problem with his cattle disappearing out of his backyard pasture and never appearing again. After appealing to the authorities, he realized that they were helpless in recovering his stolen cattle, and that he could rely only upon himself to solve the problem. One day an idea came to him to place some form of hidden identification upon his cattle. After much thought he came up with a solution. By making a small incision in the hollow of the hock, he was able to insert a dime with a specific date on it. The cut soon healed, and each of his animals was now worth ten cents more per head.

Weeks passed uneventfully until one day he returned home from a fishing trip and discovered two steers were missing. For the next two days he traveled the country roads asking people if they had seen his steers. One of his contacts tipped him off to look at the local kill yard. Frank traveled over to the butcher's place and there identified his two bovines in a crowded corral. Without accosting the owner of the facility, he retrieved the sheriff, brought him to the butcher's pens, and then confronted the owner with the allegation that he had stolen his cattle.

The butcher indignantly denied the charge, stating smugly that he had bought the cattle a long time ago, and, in fact, they had his brand on them. Frank glanced at the fresh brands, then looked the man squarely in the eye and said calmly, "Well, you've thought of everything but one thing." He went on to explain to the sheriff that all of his cows had a dime encased under the skin of their left hock. After naming the exact dates on the dimes, the two steers were run into a chute and the dimes were surgically excised. Following a police investigation, the butcher was subsequently arrested and prosecuted and confessed to having stolen many cattle over the years.

Self-reliance means we exercise the power of our mental faculties and physical capabilities in acquiring the necessary commodities of life and in the resolution of the common problems associated with mortality. As with all true principles,

Satan has devised both counterfeit and opposing principles to confuse and mislead. While the Lord's servants quietly teach the correct doctrine of self-reliance, Satan proclaims the doctrines of self-sufficiency and subordination. As members of God's kingdom on earth it is imperative that we recognize and expose Lucifer's teachings for the falsehoods that they are.

A dairyman in Beaver, Utah, once had a cow that was brighter than the ordinary bovine. As she got older, she got smarter. After a period of time she taught herself to open gates by sticking her head through the fence and nudging the latch on the other side until it released the gate. In the milking parlor she learned to get more grain by butting her head against the grain hopper. Her owner had to become more and more ingenious in devising ways to keep his gates locked and his intelligent cow out of trouble.

One evening a careless employee did not secure the corral gate tightly. During the night, the old cow picked the lock and was soon prowling around the farmyard. Her keen sense of smell led her to the large grain bin which housed the barley. She went to the door and tested the latch with her nose. This latch would have befuddled the cow of normal intellect, but held no secrets for this intellectually superior one. Soon the door to the grain bin swung open and she began to gorge. This time, however, she outsmarted herself. By morning she was dead. The large amount of grain she had consumed caused an excess of lactic acid to build up in her stomach, which dropped her body pH so low that her blood could no longer carry oxygen. She was a victim of her own appetite and of knowledge devoid of wisdom.

The prophet Jacob recognized this same attitude in his day and tackled the problem with these prophetic words.

"O that cunning plan of the evil one! O the vainness, and the frailties, and the foolishness of men!

When they are learned they think they are wise, and they hearken not unto the counsel of God, for they set it aside, supposing they know of themselves, wherefore, their wisdom is foolishness and it profiteth them not. And they shall perish.

"But to be learned is good if they hearken unto the counsels of God" (2 Ne, 9:28-29).

Satan's counterfeit doctrine of self-sufficiency teaches man that he alone has power to control his own destiny. Unlike self-reliance, which is divinely centered, self-sufficiency is egocentric with the basic theorem that man conquers by his own genius and cunning. This secular philosophy of egoism leads to vanity and pride and denies the relevance of divine influence.

My brother-in-law has an uncle named Randall who formerly lived and worked in the backcountry of Wyoming. During that time Randall was a respected cowpoke, calm, competent, and pragmatic. Unfortunately, he had a love for whiskey, and all of those fine qualities were negated when he drank. Late one night, after an evening of heavy drinking, he left his friends at a small country bar and headed back to the ranch where he was employed. The horse he was riding picked up the trail home and was moving across country at a snappy trot when suddenly he gave a snort and pulled up stiff-legged.

Equally surprised, but going the opposite direction, was a large grizzly bear that had also come to a halt. Since they occupied the same trail one of them needed to detour, but neither the bear nor the cowboy budged as they stood and stared at each other. Drunk as he was, Randall's mental clarity was dimmed, and instead of being frightened by the confrontation he grew angry at the bear's stubborn insistence that the trail belonged to him. After calling the bear an uncomplimentary name, he loosened his lariat from off his saddle and shook out a big loop. With the dexterity that comes from long practice, he easily dabbed the loop around the bear's head.

"I've got you now!" Randall shouted drunkenly and defiantly as he dallied the rope around his horn and signaled for his horse to back up. As the rope tightened around his neck the bear roared angrily, and then, with deceptive speed and deadly intent, charged the skittish horse and the drunken cowboy. The bear's earnest charge unnerved the already petrified horse that pivoted on his hocks and ran. No matter how fast he ran, however, he was still attached to the bear, and was only able to escape after Randall sobered enough to cut the rope with a knife.

If he could, Satan would attach all of us to the rope we so cleverly throw over his head in the name of self-sufficiency. Those who hold to this philosophy arrogantly believe they can manipulate people and forces onto the path of their self-interest by the force of personal influence. While relying strictly upon the power of our own mental and physical faculties may gratify our pride and vain ambition, it leaves little room for the stirrings of humility and the intervention of divine assistance at times of real crisis.

By contrast, self-reliance teaches us to faithfully do all that is within our spiritual, mental and physical power to resolve our challenges, and then, when we have exercised our personal resources, we may righteously ask for a divine lifeline to be extended to us. As we grab hold of this rope, we feel the gentle pull of the Holy Ghost directing us along paths we could not find on our own.

Another of Satan's skillful ploys is the use of subordination. He teaches that we should subordinate or turn the responsibility for our spiritual, emotional, mental, and physical welfare over to those who are wiser or more powerful than ourselves. As we enter into this compliantly dependent state, we gradually become incapable of willful volition. Unfortunately, although we have lost the power of independent decision, we still pay the penalty for our deeds. Like a wave of the sea, we are driven with the wind and tossed. In a worst-case scenario, the Book of Mormon warns that as we slide gradually and easily under the influence of sin, we become bound by Satan's flaxen cords until, like puppets, we are entirely dependent upon his commands. He becomes the master, and we become the slave.

A folk legend tells the story of a man who ventured into the heart of the Okefenokee Swamp to trap wild hogs in order to send them to market. He was warned that the hogs were cunning and dangerous and too wise to fall for any scheme of entrapment. The would-be trapper smiled, purchased a truck-load of corn and disappeared into the swamp.

The first day he spread corn around the swamp and waited to see what the hogs would do. A few of the younger hogs stopped and curiously sniffed the corn. As they nibbled at the strange food, they discovered that it was good to eat. Each day the corn was deposited on the ground and more and more of the younger hogs ate it, realizing that it was much easier to eat the free meal than to grub for roots. Eventually even the old hogs lost some of their skepticism and began to rely on the corn as a source of food.

Soon the man stopped spreading the corn randomly, and concentrated its distribution at a central location. The clearing he selected for feeding initially created a sense of insecurity among the hogs. They were reluctant to enter the clearing since it offered no shelter from predators and was a nuisance to travel that far off their normal trails. At first only the very young hogs came, but gradually all the hogs decided it was easier to come to the clearing and eat the free corn than to hunt for their own food. They still subsidized their diet with roots and nuts and snakes, and were still free to come and go, but the corn was a delicious and easy meal and they became accustomed to staying closer to the clearing.

One day the man placed fence posts in the ground. The hogs were immediately suspicious of this strange addition to their surroundings, but soon rationalized that the posts did not hurt them and the corn was still in its customary place. After a week had passed the hogs entered the clearing one morning and discovered that a rail was attached at the bottom of the posts. This was inconvenient, but did not hamper their independence, and they easily jumped the rail or went through the open gates to get their free meal.

On a certain day the man failed to place corn on the ground. The hogs were very upset, and squealed and grunted their displeasure because they were no longer used to finding their own food. When they returned the following day they saw that another rail had been added to the fence posts, but they also saw that corn was again on the ground. They clambered over the rails or ran noisily through the gates, and greedily satisfied their hunger.

The hogs hardly noticed when a third rail was placed on the fence posts. Corn was on the ground, the gates were open, and they could come and go as they pleased. Life was good, the living was easy, and they did not suffer the inconveniences which accompanied constantly searching for food and shelter. Then one morning when their appetite for breakfast was at a fevered pitch, they stampeded through the gates without seeing a high fourth rail that had been added to the fence posts. They devoured their corn, grunted for more, and failed to perceive that the gates had been closed and locked behind them.

The doctrine of self-reliance is fundamental in the body of truth, which is the gospel of good news. The Lord wishes us to become like him and is willing to help us in this quest but leaves the burden of self-initiative squarely upon our shoulders. Satan, on the other hand, is eager to feed us the manna of unrighteousness and gradually subordinate our will to his by the gradual erosion of our agency through subtle and crafty means. He wants us to be seduced by the easiness of the way and the immediate gratification of the appetite.

Nephi summarized the essence of true self-reliance and the partnership it creates with the Lord. Listen to his words.

"I will go and do the things which the Lord hath commanded, for I know that the Lord giveth no commandments unto the children of men, save he shall prepare a way for them that they may accomplish the thing which he commandeth them." (1 Ne. 3:7)

"And I was led by the Spirit, not knowing beforehand the things which I should do.

"Nevertheless I went forth. . ." (1 Ne. 4:6-7).

We, too, must go forth, perhaps not knowing beforehand the things we should do, but relying on the Spirit to guide us along the path of eternal life.

Chapter 9

No Other Success

The October afternoon was hot even by Arizona standards, and perspiration rolled down the back of my shirt as I stood under the full glare of the sun. I had agreed to meet Freddy Rodriquez, who was a new convert to the church, outside of the Institute building on the University of Arizona campus. The class bell had just rung, and students swarmed around us as we discussed an item of business. Over the clamor of students scurrying to make their next class, a loud roaring sound intruded upon our senses and drowned out all other noise. The high decibel roaring overhead made it impossible to hear each other even at a shout.

We looked up in the sky to determine the cause of the deafening sound. A fighter jet from Davis Monthan Air Force base was on a low trajectory above our heads. While we stared in amazement, we heard a loud bang and watched incredulously as the pilot ejected out of the plane. Seconds later, the jet bellied over, narrowly missed a campus high-rise building, and then in a thunderous explosion smashed into the ground. Billows of black smoke poured out of the burning plane and lifted into the air like a signal plume. Drawn by morbid curiosity we sprinted toward the crash site.

Almost instantaneously the air was filled with the ominous screech and wail of sirens as police, fire, and medical authorities all jockeyed into position to bring order to a chaotic situation. By the time we arrived, the whole area had been cordoned off by trained emergency personnel who were frantically trying to pierce the thick clouds of smoke and determine casualties.

For a moment, transport yourself away from the scene of this tragic airplane crash and picture yourself in complete darkness; a darkness so thick that it is palpable. You have just survived a catastrophic earthquake, and in the aftermath, in the darkness, you cannot be sure that any of your family or friends have survived. Since you cannot see, you must grope your way around your surroundings, and rely upon your peripheral senses. The din and noise is continuous, and, though not deafening, there is no escape from the doleful lamentation of the people around you. Your own anxiety and grief is an insuperable burden, and after three days of this nerve-racking bedlam you feel as though you are at the edge of an emotional and mental chasm.

At this critical juncture, you detect an unusual sound. At first you think you may have imagined it. As you strain your faculties in an attempt to identify the source and direction of the sound, you notice that all around you the mournful howling of human emotion is gradually diminishing. Suddenly you realize that the sound you hear is that of a human voice speaking, and it is coming from somewhere above you. It is not a harsh voice, neither is it a loud voice, but notwithstanding it being a small voice, it pierces you to the center. Your body begins to tremble and your heart palpitates wildly for intuitively you realize that it is the voice of God. When finally the world around you grows silent, when all outside distractions have been muted, then, and only then, are you able to comprehend the voice.

Despite superior advances in communication technology, ours is a society that more closely resembles the world of Babel than the city of Enoch. We live in a time defined by its frenetic, high-decibel, unremittent noise rather than its clarity of thought or enunciation of ideals. With so many voices calling us, with the harsh din of the world thundering in our ears, sometimes it is difficult to recognize the soft-spoken voice of Deity. If we lend an ear to the incessantly loud and specious philosophies of men, we can easily be distracted from the quiet voice of truth and reason. Like a jet engine roaring overhead, worldly standards of right and wrong demand attention, but hinder introspective examination. On the other hand, when the Lord speaks by the still, small voice of the Spirit, it is the chords of the heart that respond. It is always from within, and not from without, that we recognize truth.

One of the comforting gospel truths revealed to us in these latter days is that the family unit is eternal. These mortal familial relationships which mean so much to us now, can potentially cross the boundary of death and be enjoyed from everlasting to everlasting. Because our existence in the next life is both a reflection and restoration of those things which were important to us here, a prophet of God in this dispensation has warned, "No other success can compensate for failure in the home."

With such a pleasant potential before us, it is not surprising that Satan attempts to drown out the soft voice of the spirit with the overhead screech of a dying jet. If he can divert our attention and make us lose our concentration, then the Father's plan for eternal families can be thwarted, and Satan will have won some measure of vindication. Despite prophetic warnings, sometimes we are drawn to the sound of the siren; we rush to the scene of the accident, only to discover belatedly that we are not the spectators but the victims of the crash.

One evening, in my growing up years, my family went up to the Santa Catalina Mountains outside Tucson to cook dinner. While we roasted our hotdogs over a fire, Duke, my German Shepherd dog, left our family in search of adventure. Soon after disappearing, his ferocious barking signaled that he had found it. A short time later he trotted back into camp. Instead of his normally proud carriage, there was a furtive, tail-between-the-legs look about him. There was also an unmistakably pungent aroma radiating in nauseating waves from off his hide. Duke had been "skunked."

Those sheltered individuals who have never sniffed the delicate fragrance of skunk at close range will be unable to appreciate the rest of the story. Perfumed as he was, Duke was having a hard time finding a friend. This was unfortunate because he desperately wanted one. Under the circumstances, the family mutually agreed to abort the cookout and head home. This presented a problem because we had come in our family sedan with Duke riding in the backseat with us kids. By parental decree it was decided that Duke would have to ride in the trunk of the car. Since we were concerned that he might become alarmed at this unorthodox mode of travel, and exit out of the trunk prematurely, it was also determined that someone would need to ride with him. There were no volunteers. In the absence of volunteers, the task devolved upon his rightful owner.

As an unhappy conscript I complained bitterly, but piled in the trunk with my dog. Duke and I made a pitiful pair riding home side by side across dusty, desert roads. I held him tightly so that he would not jump out onto the road and be injured, and he reciprocated my concern by constantly licking my face with his tongue. By the time we reached home we were indistinguishable in terms of odor and misery.

Like riding home with a skunky dog, there are times when we as individuals cannot shirk our family duties without endangering the long-term health of the family unit. Regardless of how inconvenient or odoriferous the task may appear, as mothers and fathers we cannot abrogate our God-given responsibility to continuously "train up a child in the way he should go." Abandoning our children at the first sign of trouble is tantamount to kicking them out the back of the family sedan onto the roads of life without a map or compass. It is unlikely that they will find their way home.

In the 88th section of the Doctrine and Covenants, the Lord gives us precise directions home. His map instructs us to organize ourselves in such a manner that our houses may be worthy of the presence of God and reflect the principles of prayer, fasting, faith, learning, and order.

A house of prayer

It was a normal sacrament meeting. I was sitting on the stand as the bishop of the Emmett, Idaho, Third Ward. The sacrament was being passed. All was quiet except for the usual light chatter of children's voices. I was concentrating on other thoughts, not paying attention to the background noise, when I heard a cry that jerked me out of my reverie. I knew instantly that it was the cry of Emily, my three-year-old daughter. I looked down in the congregation and spotted my family. My impulse was correct. I knew my little girl's voice above all others and despite all others.

By the same token, our Heavenly Father recognizes first those voices he hears most frequently. As a family, we should hold prayers night and morning. As individuals, we should cultivate the habit of private daily prayers. In addition to our regular prayers, the Savior instructs us that we should always have a prayer in our hearts that we might avoid the temptations of the devil.

Spiritually healthy families that strive to do what is right know that the blessings of heaven are contingent upon our asking for them. Even the most difficult circumstances and problems are not insoluble when the prayer of faith is unitedly directed toward our Heavenly Father's merciful ear.

"For the eyes of the Lord are over the righteous, and his ears are open unto their prayers: but the face of the Lord is against them that do evil" (1 Peter 3:12).

However, there is a sickness in our society that threatens to rob even the healthiest families of vitality. It is not a disease of body, but a pathology of the heart and mind. Its symptoms are easily diagnosed by the priority of our lifestyle. In a world where the highly-infectious craving for material possessions has displaced spiritual yearnings, and where the love of money has replaced natural affection, it is easy to be exposed to this contagious illness. The Lord, in his role as spiritual physician, gives us a remedy, a cure, and a preventive antidote to this spiritual toxin.

"Pray always, and I will pour out my Spirit upon you, and great shall be your blessing—yea, even more than if you should obtain treasures of earth and corruptibleness to the extent thereof" (D&C 19:38).

A house of fasting

When I was a teacher in the Aaronic Priesthood, one of my fellow quorum members was thrown off a motorcycle and severely injured. As his life hung in the balance, I fasted and prayed in his behalf. When my friend died as a result of his injuries, a feeling of peace assured me that the Lord's will had been exercised.

In the fifty-ninth section of the Doctrine and Covenants, the Lord promises blessings of peace and joy, and blessings from the abundance of the earth to all who properly keep the law of the fast. Fasting and prayer go hand-in-glove like faith and works. Those families that practice the principle of the fast will have enhanced faith, and more effectual works as a consequence of fasting and prayer. In a world of almost universal cynicism toward things spiritual, family members will learn that the unadvertised power of God is vastly superior to the highly publicized powers of modern science and technology.

A house of faith

One summer, between college semesters, I was hired by the University of Arizona to aid in calf research being conducted by my father. The experiment was designed to determine the importance of the quality of colostrum milk in the passive immune status of neonatal calves. Our experimental protocol was to collect a blood sample from a calf as soon as it was born and then remove it from its mother before it could suckle. We would then feed it a prearranged quantity and predetermined quality of colostrum. If the colostrum had high enough levels of immunoglobulins and was fed within six hours of birth, it would protect the calf against the debilitating effect of disease.

Faith is a spiritual colostrum which when imbibed protects us against the harmful bacteria of fear and doubt. It is the substance of things hoped for, the evidence of things not seen. As one of the fundamental doctrines of the gospel, faith is taught by precept but learned only by practice. Active, vibrant faith in Christ transforms mundane commandments into exhilarating spiritual experiments.

When I was a boy I witnessed a frightening scene. We were swimming as a family in a friend's swimming pool. My mother had been having spells of vertigo, but was carefully swimming with us. Vertigo is symptomized by periods of intense dizziness brought on by disorders of the inner ear. While we were swimming, Mom submerged under the water. When one of us kids noticed that she was struggling at the bottom of the pool, we yelled an alarm. My father dove into the pool and pulled her out. After being brought to the surface, she explained that when she went under water she became dizzy and disoriented, and lost her sense of direction. She had no clue which direction led to the surface of the water.

The cardinal rule of faith is that it must have direction. Faith as a stand-alone principle will not stand up. Faith in the Lord Jesus Christ is the only faith that leads to salvation. Faith in Christ encompasses his person, his actions, and his doctrine. True faith is a reflection of his divine attributes. Consequently, it is not a sword to be brandished at unbelievers but rather a shield to guard us against their fiery darts. Putting on the shield of faith allows us to be protected by the whole armor of God.

Tom Kuechenberg was an Orthodox Jew. He became attracted to the Church because of the people he knew who were LDS. His curiosity about what made Mormons unique caused him to investigate the doctrines of the church. He found the discussions fascinating from a philosophical point of view but refused to take them seriously as a spiritual perspective. He dogmatically resisted praying for a witness of our teachings if it meant asking in the name of Christ.

One day he was reading the Book of Mormon in solitude. Something impressed him beyond the ordinary, and he decided to undertake the experiment we had urged him to try. He knelt beside his bed and, in the name of Christ, called upon Heavenly Father to reveal to him the truth of the Book of Mormon. His simple act of faith yielded a powerful manifestation from the Holy Ghost. Later he remarked to us that his whole soul felt as if it were on fire.

Alma defines faith as a hope in things which are not seen, but which, nevertheless, are true. This truth is self-evident; without some knowledge of God our Father, and his son, Jesus Christ, we cannot exercise even a scintilla of faith in them. The apostle Paul in his epistle to the Roman's tells us this:

> "So then faith cometh by hearing, and hearing by the word of God" (Romans 10:17).

The scriptures are a recording of God's instructions to man, and as such, reveal to us our eternal possibilities. The word of God has been likened to an iron rod that leads us inexorably along the path of faith to the fruit of eternal life. By Alma's definition, faith requires us to step where we cannot see. The path to eternal life is lined with blind obstacles intended to trip us and test our resolve. Only those who grasp the word of God will traverse this path with any degree of confidence.

One summer I lived with my grandparents on their small dairy farm in Kanosh, Utah. One of my responsibilities was the daily driving of the cattle to and from the pasture. My grandfather initially went with me to teach me the hidden dangers lurking along the mile route. He taught me to observe the lead cows to see that they didn't swerve out onto the main road and take the whole herd into traffic. I was also to watch out for dogs or other distractions that might frighten the cows and cause them to run off.

At first my new responsibility was exciting, and the duties of the job gripped my attention like a vise. Time went by, and day after plodding day I delivered the cattle back and forth from the pasture without mishap. One sultry August afternoon my thoughts began to wander and soar. I became oblivious to the cattle walking in front of me. Suddenly I became aware of the fact that thirty head of Holstein cows were stampeding toward me, and that I was about to join company with the other trampled remnants of the herd's passage. My imminent danger paralyzed me with fear. I could not move a muscle. As I stood stupidly watching the cows charge me, I could almost visualize my headstone:

"Here lies Kevin Stott.

Trampled by cows.

May he rest in one piece."

The thought of such an ignominious end galvanized me into action. With my stockman's whip whistling and popping in their astonished faces, I managed to stop the herd of cows before being pulverized.

Unlike belief, faith in Christ is not passive and can only be expressed by mental or physical action on our part, which action is made possible because of our confidence in Christ and his promises. James, the brother of Jesus, explains that our works of righteousness define the line between passive belief and active faith. After all, he concludes, "the devils also believe and tremble." When our belief is transformed through faith into active participation in the building of God's kingdom on earth, then we receive a dispensation of power from Heaven. This power is manifested in our lives by the gifts of the Spirit.

A house of learning

The story is told of a young boy growing up in the ranching community of Eager, Arizona. As his only means of transportation, he rode his horse five miles to school. His father was a rancher by profession and had never received a formal education. Because of that deficit in his life, he took schooling seriously and wanted all of his children to get as much education as they could.

One day this young man came riding home from school at noon. When his dad saw him ride up he left his lunch, walked outside, and asked him what in the world he was doing home. The boy replied that his teacher, old Mr. Spencer, had kicked him out of school. When his father asked why Mr. Spencer had kicked him out, the boy could not give an explanation. He simply didn't know why. His father puzzled over this riddle for a minute and then told his son to get back on his horse and they would go straighten the problem out.

When they arrived back at the schoolhouse, the father beckoned for the schoolmaster to come outside. When Mr. Spencer had complied with his request the father asked him, "Jim, why'd ya kick my boy out of class?"

"Well, I kicked him out for smartin' off," came the reply. "When I asked him who signed the Declaration of Independence, he said he didn't know, but he hadn't done it."

The boy's father nodded his head solemnly, thanked the

teacher, mounted his horse, and rode off with his son following closely behind him. Not a word was spoken on the ride home, but when the boy dismounted to open the ranch gate his father leaned over in his saddle and said, "Now you little scamp, did you or did you not sign that dang fool thing, whatever it was?"

In modern scripture the Lord emphasizes his desire for us to be an enlightened people with these words:

"And as all have not faith, seek ye diligently and teach one another words of wisdom; yea, seek ye out of the best books words of wisdom; seek learning, even by study and also by faith." (D&C 88:118).

Education is a necessary step toward godhood because "the glory of God is intelligence, or, in other words, light and truth" (D&C 93:36). As parents, we should foster an environment in our home which is conducive to both gospel and secular scholarship. Our responsibility also extends to teaching our children to differentiate between trivial facts and saving knowledge. As Jacob, the brother of Nephi, reminds us, "to be learned is good if we hearken unto the counsels of God." Educated individuals who deny the relevancy of God's wisdom are always learning but never able to come to a knowledge of the truth. Intelligence, which is a gift of God, allows us to place facts in their proper order and visualize things as they really are.

A friend of mine spent years delivering the mail in the rural area of Gem County, Idaho. One day while delivering mail along the highway below the Black Canyon Dam, he witnessed a guinea hen wander away from one of the small farms bordering the highway and get hit by a passing motorist. Before dying, the mortally wounded hen emitted a loud squawk and then flopped over on the blacktop. Her dying shriek aroused the attention of six of her former friends who came flapping across the road to learn what the commotion was all about. As the guinea hens congregated around their fallen comrade they deduced that she was dead but couldn't figure out what had killed her. Just then a logging truck came barreling over the top of the hill. Even in their final moments they were always learning, but never able to come to a knowledge of the truth.

It was in the tenth grade that I became acquainted with Posedly. He wasn't tall, or large, or muscular, or handsome. Posedly was smart. He had black hair, black glasses, and an abnormally large nose. He was quiet, weird, made excellent grades, and was known to talk to himself. He was eccentric enough that his classmates didn't deride him overtly—only behind his back. I did not make fun of him at all. For some reason he considered me his friend, perhaps because I respected his individuality. Generally, he was unconcerned about other people's opinions of him.

Posedly read a book about Ty Cobb, the great Detroit Tigers baseball player who competed in the early 1900s. This book captured his interest and fired his imagination. Ty Cobb was the greatest base-stealer the game had ever known. After reading this book, his new ambition was to be like Cobb.

He went out for the high school baseball team and made it. In the afternoons before practice began, I would go to the batting cage and take my swings. While I hit I would watch Posedly practice by himself on the diamond. He was outfitted in a strange uniform that he had contrived to enhance his sliding practice: old Levis with leather stitched to the knees and backside and a white T-shirt over the top.

He would pose ten feet off first base, glare at an imaginary pitcher, knees bent slightly, arms akimbo, and then suddenly he would sprint toward second base. The area around second base would disappear in a cloud of dust as he plowed a long furrow in the dirt. Posedly would then emerge out of the dust, cough once or twice, pat the back of his pants, and then his lips would move as he chastened himself or congratulated himself on the quality of his slide. He would then walk slowly back to first base where the whole pantomime began again.

Through his self-discipline and aptitude for detail, Posedly mastered the art of stealing bases. He was quick, and clever, and had perfected the standup, hook, and belly slides. In practice he studied our pitcher's moves and knew what size lead to take and when to run. He could have become the greatest base-stealer our school had ever known—but he did not. I led the team in stolen bases that year. The problem was, he had never learned to hit. Consequently, he never got on base.

While all education in truth has merit, to transform knowledge to wisdom, it is obvious that a house of learning must be built from the ground up, using fundamental truths as our building blocks. Without the foundational facts of the plan of salvation to systemize and give order to our accumulated knowledge, we may never get the opportunity to utilize it for our own benefit.

A house of order

In our dispensation the Lord has declared:

"Behold, mine house is a house of order, saith the Lord God, and not a house of confusion" (D&C 132:8).

In the *Proclamation to the World*, the Lord has set forth the proper organization of the family unit.

"By divine design, fathers are to preside over their families in love and righteousness and are responsible to provide the necessities of life and protection for their families. Mothers are primarily responsible for the nurture of their children. In these sacred responsibilities, fathers and mothers are obligated to help one another as equal partners. Disability, death, or other circumstances may necessitate individual adaptations."

As parents in Zion, ours is the solemn obligation to establish a house of order where eternal ambitions can be realized, where children can be nurtured under the influence of the Holy Spirit, and where faith and testimony abide. As we organize our families in the way that our Heavenly Father has prescribed, we can successfully compensate for all evil influences designed to create failure in the home.

Chapter 10

Do Good Continually

It was known as the Zoramite Mission. As mission president, he had witnessed many conversions through the powerful influence of the Holy Ghost, but he had also seen large numbers of people turn their hearts away from the truth, and passionately persecute the true believers. Through the good times and the bad, he was sustained by his faith in Jesus Christ. His faith was tested to its supreme level when one of his chosen missionaries was tempted by a harlot and fell into moral sin. That missionary was his own son. As a concerned parent, he privately took his son aside and taught him one of the basic doctrines of salvation:

"Do not suppose, because it has been spoken concerning restoration, that ye shall be restored from sin to happiness. Behold I say unto you, wickedness never was happiness" (Alma 41:10).

Then Alma concluded his interview with his wayward son Corianton with this sapient advice:

"Therefore, my son, see that you are merciful unto your brethren; deal justly, judge righteously, and do good continually;. . ." (Alma 41:14).

It is this counsel, to do good continually, that pulls at the heart and conscience of all who have sinned and fallen short of the glory of God.

The night was black, and the shadows cast by the overhanging trees intensified the darkness. Almost invisible amongst those trees knelt a solitary man. His face was indistinguishable in the blackness, but his voice, as he talked aloud, revealed a great anguish of soul. Suddenly the voice stopped, interrupted by an intruding noise far below him on the hill. He raised his head. Coming toward him were the scintillating lights of hand-held torches accompanied by the shouts of a large contingent of men. Despite his best efforts to secure a private sanctum, the mob had found him.

He pushed himself slowly up from his kneeling position and walked down the hill to meet them. He was not afraid; cowardice was a trait that simply was not a part of him. As he came in view of the riffraff who were intent on murdering him, three of his closest friends emerged quietly from the shadows of nearby trees. As the rabble approached the four men, the leader of the mob vociferously demanded to know the whereabouts of the person they were seeking. The brave man from the hill stepped forward and acknowledged that he was the one that they sought. He then pointed to his three friends and said, "Let these go their way."

As the bloodthirsty crowd eagerly surged forward to apprehend their man, one of his friends drew his sword from a sheath and with a powerful downward stroke sliced an ear off the nearest ruffian. The craven mob backed off in stunned silence. They had not anticipated armed resistance, and the fisherman's muscular physique gave evidence that he was capable of giving them a fight. In the quiet interlude that followed, only one voice was heard:

> "Then said Jesus unto Peter, Put up thy sword into the sheath: the cup which my Father hath given me, shall I not drink it?" (John 18:11).

> ". . .for all they that take the sword shall perish with the sword" (Matt. 26:52).

Then Jesus touched the afflicted ear and healed it.

In our inverted world where good is spoken of as evil and evil is considered the ultimate good, where darkness is light, and light is darkness, even egotism and selfishness pose as legitimate surrogates for altruism. In such a bewildering world there are so few examples of one who does good continually. As we look back in time to the magnanimous life of our Savior Jesus Christ, we see that his response in every situation and to every provocation was to do good. Even in life-threatening circumstances, charity never failed him.

For the rest of us, charity does not come that easily. So frequently in life we flunk the daily character tests placed before us, not because charity failed us, but because we failed to have charity. Of all the mortal subjects we can study in this probationary period, mastery of the discipline of charity will bring us closer to Christ than the sum total of all other earthly curriculum. As we learn from the example of the Son of God, we see that his charity was physically manifested by his habit of doing good continually. That enduring habit of doing good can be ingrained into our own character if we practice patience, kindness, and virtue.

During the summer which I spent with my grandparents on their farm, I worked hard, and I played hard. My play involved riding my pony, as well as any sheep or calves that I could catch. One of the animals that I wanted to ride was a little Black Angus calf. Every day I would try to get close enough to rope him, and every day he would evade capture.

One day I was walking toward the milk barn when I glanced over to the calf pen and noticed the Angus steer stretched out in the sun sleeping soundly. I cautiously climbed the fence and tiptoed to the slumbering calf. Before he could awake I straddled him, and with a satisfied grin on my face waited for the fun to begin. The calf awoke to find an irksome human being clinging to his back. Instead of standing up and frantically bucking, he lay as still as a statue. I waited patiently for him to move. He waited patiently for me to leave. As boy and bovine played chicken in the barnyard, I was the first to flinch. This is stupid, I thought, he's never going to move.

Impatiently I stood up. Underneath me, the calf felt a release of my weight, and shrewdly chose that moment to explode into action. He jumped up, and with an athletic maneuver tucked his head between his front legs and then kicked his hind legs vigorously over his back. Caught off guard, I was catapulted high into the sky. After doing a lazy somersault in the air, my flying career ended abruptly with a crash in the muck surrounding the water tank. I raised my head out of the manure so that I could breath, wiped my eyes clear so that I could see, licked my lips so that I could cuss (that was a mistake), and then walked dejectedly to the house. The aroma emanating from my clothes was so pervasive that my grandmother insisted that I stand outside while she sprayed me down. Having just learned a vital lesson in patience, I mutely submitted to the indignity of the garden hose.

Patience can be acquired through a variety of methods. Regardless of the method of acquisition, patience is an integral part of doing good, because, as the prophet Mormon informs us, charity suffereth long. The Apostle Paul amplifies that theme in his epistle to the saints in Rome, as he describes who it is that will receive eternal life.

> *"To them who by patient continuance in well doing seek for glory and honour and immortality, eternal life. . ."* (Romans 2:7).

Charity not only suffereth long, but it is kind. By definition, kindness is to be thoughtful, gentle, tender, compassionate, and loving. It is to have a benevolent disposition with an innate propensity to do good whenever the opportunity arises.

Brigham Young demonstrated his kindness on many occasions. Once, B.F. Grant, the fourteen-year-old orphaned son of Jedediah M. Grant, made his way to Salt Lake City. Brigham invited him into his office, and while shaking his hand was surprised to discover a thick callous covering it.

"My boy, what kind of work are you doing?" Brigham asked.

"I am unloading coal and chopping wood," came the reply.

"Isn't it pretty heavy work, shoveling coal and chopping wood, for a boy of your age?"

"No, sir, I have been used to hard work all of my life."

"Wouldn't you like to have something easier than your present work, for instance, a position in a store?"

"I haven't got sense enough to work in a store," came the dispirited reply.

"What do you mean by that?"

"I can neither read nor write."

Tears of compassion rolled down Brigham's cheeks and he said tenderly, "My boy, come and live with me; I will give you a home; I will clothe you; I will send you to school; and you can work during the vacation for me."

When patience and kindness are yoked to virtue, doing good becomes a natural extension of our personality and a reflection of our spirit. Virtue means to think no evil, to rejoice not in iniquity, but to rejoice in the truth. Virtuous thoughts are significant not only because of the absence of evil but also because of the presence of good. Charitable actions begin with virtuous thoughts, and when both are brought to fruition then we are promised confidence in the presence of God.

In the last agonizing moments of Jesus' life, when he had suffered far beyond our mortal comprehension, he looked down from high on the cross and saw his mother Mary. Putting aside the all-encompassing pain that racked his physical body, his thoughts, always virtuous, turned to her welfare. Seeing John, his beloved disciple, standing next to her, he said,

"Woman, behold thy son!" Then to John he said, "Behold thy mother!" And when that last good act had been accomplished, Jesus bowed his head and surrendered his spirit, and by so doing became the keeper of the gate leading to eternal life.

"O then, my beloved brethren, come unto the Lord, the Holy One. Remember that his paths are righteous. Behold, the way for man is narrow, but it lieth in a straight course before him, and the keeper of the gate is the Holy One of Israel; and he employeth no servant there; and there is none other way save it be by the gate; for he cannot be deceived, for the Lord God is his name" (2 Ne. 9:41).

On that fateful day, when you and I are brought face to face with the keeper of the gate, I envision some type of spiritual mirror, which will accurately reflect the characteristics of our souls. As we compare our acquired mortal characteristics with the immortal attributes of the Savior, he will know and we will know, with certainty, what paths we have walked in this earthly probation. As we gaze upon his compassionate countenance, we will see reflected in his eyes an understanding of the type of behavior we have extended toward our fellowman. Our souls will swell with confidence in his presence if our minds are filled with virtue, our hearts with charity, and our hands are calloused from the work of kindly deeds.

Chapter 11

Gospel Locks

On a bright, warm Sunday morning, my sixteen-year-old daughter, Riki, stayed home from church to nurse a bad cold. It was a little after nine o'clock, the family had been gone for three quarters of an hour, and Riki had been sleeping soundly when some noise in the house disturbed her slumber. She awoke and distinctly heard someone walking across the kitchen floor. Assuming that one of the family had returned unexpectedly from church, she arose to see who it was.

As she walked into the kitchen she saw that the front door was wide open. She closed and locked the door, and then looked around to determine the cause of its being open. As she did so, a subliminal feeling warned her that she was being watched from the next room. By this time her faculties were aroused to the dangers of being locked in the house with an intruder she couldn't see, but whose presence she could feel. Hastily she retreated to her bedroom where she closed the door and commenced praying with a degree of sincerity and fervency that had been absent in less urgent circumstances.

After praying, she decided that the most prudent course of action was to advance to the bathroom at the other end of the house, which had a solid lock on the door. As she prepared to carry out her plan, she listened carefully for any sounds that would reveal the whereabouts of the intruder. Her auditing was rewarded when a clicking sound was followed by a loud crash. Mustering her bravado, she broke off a wooden leg from an office chair, and armed with that formidable weapon opened her bedroom door and sprinted toward the bathroom. As she dashed past the front door she noted that it was again open to the outside. After reaching the bathroom's sanctuary, she huddled in terrified silence against the locked bathroom door until the family returned from church two hours later.

We live in perilous times; times that the apostle Paul foresaw and predicted.

> *"This know also, that in the last days perilous times shall come.*
>
> *"For men shall be lovers of their own selves, covetous, boasters, proud, blasphemers, disobedient to parents, unthankful, unholy,*
>
> *Without natural affection, trucebreakers, false accusers, incontinent, fierce, despisers of those that are good,*
>
> *"Traitors, heady, highminded, lovers of pleasures more than lovers of God;*
>
> *"Having a form of Godliness, but denying the power thereof: from such turn away.*
>
> *"For of this sort are they which creep into houses. . ."*
> (2 Tim. 3:1-6).

The intruder in our house, whoever he was, served as a frightening reminder that in these perilous last days we must be vigilant in securing our family against those influences which are capable of destroying them. One of the lessons learned from our pioneer heritage is that those families who were united in the common cause of spiritual and physical survival, and who held solidly to correct principles as a means of facilitating their survival, successfully negotiated the perilous westward migration against all outside influences. On the other hand, those families and individuals who were not committed to fundamental principles either did not make the trek or turned back before the journey's end.

A pioneer has been described as one who goes before to show the way. In our day and age, technological pioneering has cast its broad shadow over all aspects of our modern life. Technological advances occur with such frequency that we accept them impassively and without surprise. What *is* surprising is our equally passive response to societal losses in basic family values. Because society applauds and government endorses the glorification of alternative and promiscuous lifestyles, there is a definite and decided bias both institutionally and attitudinally against those who practice traditional family values. Ironically, then, to be a pioneer in our time may be as simple as being a conscientious parent.

The Christmas season of 1994 was marred only by the death of my good friend Irvin Fresh, who was 100 years old. Since I had been his former bishop, Sister Fresh asked me to conduct his funeral. I had a prior commitment to deliver a Holstein bull to a dairy in Marsing, Idaho, but felt that I could be back in time if I hurried.

After feeding the bulls that morning, I separated the one I was to deliver, weighed it, and then hollered to my wife to open the trailer gate so I could load the bull. My wife attempted to comply with my request, but had never before opened the trailer gate and was having a difficult time figuring out the mechanics of the procedure. She unlatched the sliding part of the gate before realizing that she just needed to swing the whole thing open. Once open, the bull loaded without hesitation, she slammed the gate shut, and I sped off toward Marsing.

The day was gloomy because of a cold, dense fog that obscured the sun and made driving difficult. After an anxious hour of driving I arrived at the dairy. I pulled up to the appointed pen, jumped out of the truck, and ran back to unload the bull—only to discover that it was not necessary; the bull was not there. Somewhere in transit on my fifty mile trip the unlatched sliding gate had worked its way open. The bull, demonstrating uncommon initiative and daring, unloaded himself while traveling at the speed of fifty-five miles per hour. With a bull that talented and courageous, I naturally wanted him back, but that story comes later.

Since my experience with the sliding gate, I always check the latch on my trailer after loading. Since my experience with the unbidden intruder, I always lock our house before leaving. As a church janitor while attending college, it was my duty to walk through the dark chapel at night examining door locks and window latches. During my years as a father and priesthood leader, I have also had experience with securing gospel locks and latches.

Gospel latches are the covenants we have made through priesthood ordinances and are designed to protect our families from falling out of favor with God and onto the highways of destruction. Gospel locks are Christ's commandments, and obedience to them prevents intruders from creeping into our homes and leading our children astray on dark and sinuous paths.

The word *lock* can be utilized as an acrostic to remember the four keys to gospel safety:

Look to heaven in prayer.
Open your heart with scriptures.
Close your mind to sin.
Keep your soul in obedience.

Look to heaven in prayer. In Nephi's last public exhortation to his descendants, he instructed them that the Holy Spirit teaches a man to pray while the evil spirit teaches a man not to pray. When we regularly offer prayers as a family, even if only out of a sense of duty or obligation, we invoke God's protective influence upon our homes and lock spiritual intruders out. As we offer prayers with real intent, both privately and publicly, the Lord has promised to hear us, instruct us, and sustain us in our trials, troubles, and afflictions.

After discovering that my bull had disappeared from the back of my trailer, I retraced my steps to see if I could find him. Failing in that objective, I gave up the search and made it back in time to attend the funeral I was conducting. Later that afternoon I called the sheriff's department. From them I learned that a dead Holstein bull had been reported in the Sand Hollow area along the route I had taken that morning.

That night I was distraught over my misfortune in losing the bull. Bills needed paying and my family needed the income that the bull would have brought. I presumed the bull was dead, but nevertheless prayed concerning the missing bull and our financial plight. In the middle of the night I awoke, feeling that I had overlooked something. It dawned on me that I had not spotted a dead bull at the street address the sheriff's office had quoted me.

The next morning I called the rendering company that was hired to remove dead animals, and asked them if they had picked up a dead Holstein bull at such and such street coordinates. No, they replied, they had responded to a call to pick up a dead animal there, but when the driver arrived the bull was not there as reported.

I ran out to my truck and with two of my kids sped to the reported sighting of the dead bull. As we examined the road we discovered a trail of blood going back the way we had come. We walked up the road and inquired at some of the farmhouses whether they had seen a Holstein bull walking along the road the previous day. One lady informed us that it had wandered into her yard and she had called a friend who owned a feedlot to come and get it. We thanked her for that information and drove to the feedlot. There we were given possession of our bull, wounded and hobbled up, but alive.

The Lord is willing to help us in times of trial, protect us in times of trouble, and instruct us in times of ignorance, but his blessings are predicated upon our approaching him in prayer.

Open your heart with scriptures. One day my son, Jace, then six years old, was discussing with my wife why my parents had to move off their ranch and away from the area. Laraine explained patiently that Grandpa had a bad heart, and that the work on the ranch put too much strain on him. Jace countered with the thought that we could help him with the work. My wife replied that because of other obligations we could help out only occasionally, and besides, with his heart condition, Grandpa often felt cold, which is why he had to move to a warm place such as St. George. A look of real understanding illuminated Jace's eyes and he said, "That's why he always wants me to sit on his lap—to keep him warm. But that's funny because he doesn't feel cold. Maybe he's just cold inside."

We live in a world where there are perfectly normal-looking human beings walking around who are cold inside. Spiritual warmth is felt only as we stretch our hands to the fire. By voluntarily bringing ourselves under the influence of the scriptures, we can feel the Spirit of God like a fire burning. As we hold tight to the iron rod, we are strengthened in our resolve to comport ourselves in a Christlike manner, protected from the loose latches and open doors which lead to the mists of darkness.

Close your mind to sin. One autumn I had two Holstein bulls that were over a year old and of disagreeable temperaments. All the other bulls I had on the place were younger and more amiable in their social outlook. These two bulls occupied their own pen, which they guarded tenaciously. To enter their pen was both foolhardy and dangerous.

One day I was feeding the baby calves when I glanced up in

time to see the bigger of the two bulls butt his head up against one of his pen's fence panels and knock it down. He then jumped over the fallen fence and exited in the direction of the public lake that borders our property. My heart skipped several beats as I envisioned fishermen jumping into the water to save themselves from a crazed bull rampaging along the shore. With that visionary incentive, I grabbed a stock whip and sprinted to head the bull off before he could hook a fisherman. I ran in front of the bull, turned him around, and drove him back past the fence he had knocked down. Once back on our property I waited for reinforcements. The first one to join me was the other bull.

I was in a predicament. I could not fix the fence and guard it at the same time. Since I stood as the last bastion between civilization and mass destruction, leaving the gap was not an option. While the bulls pawed the dirt in front of me and made threatening gestures, I prayed for help. At this critical juncture my son Clay walked out to the calf barn from the house. I alerted him to my situation and requested his assistance. Together we worked out a strategy. Clay would hold the bulls at bay while I retrieved a steel fence panel to plug the gap.

I had gone only about thirty yards when I heard Clay yell. One of the bulls had pinned him against a portion of the fence that was still upright and was attempting to give him a massage. Clay was beating the bull over the head with a whip, but his exertions were ineffective in dampening the bull's ardor. I ran back, leaped the fence, and using greater powers of persuasion whacked the bull on top of the head with a wooden club. He wisely backed off. Together we concluded to drive the bulls out of the pen before attempting further repairs, and working cautiously, secured them in a small holding pen.

After repairing the fence, we went to retrieve the bulls. Much to our consternation the holding pen was empty and the gate was open. Just then we heard a frenzied shouting coming from the back of the house. We ran to the backyard where we came upon a bizarre scene. My wife was bounding up and down on the trampoline while our two missing bulls circled her with perplexed looks on their faces. From the living room window she had seen the bulls push open the gate in the holding pen. When she went outside to shoo them back, the bulls chased her into the backyard where she narrowly escaped by jumping onto the trampoline. By jumping high in the air whenever a bull approached her, she was able to keep them baffled and at bay. However, she was not a happy jumper.

Closing our mind to sin is like surrounding ourselves with a good strong fence. Not only does it keep bad things out, it keeps good things in. As parents we need to surround our families with a stout spiritual fence, keeping wholesome influences in and evil influences out. This means that we secure our gates and do not allow any uninvited guests to barge into our homes unexpectedly, via unsupervised television, videos, or Internet.

The prophet Mormon understood the difference a strong fence and a secure gate meant to the spiritual lives of his people. In addition, he understood implicitly which side of the fence the bull was on.

> "Wherefore, all things which are good cometh of God; and that which is evil cometh of the devil; for the devil is an enemy unto God, and fighteth against him continually, and inviteth and enticeth to sin, and to do that which is evil continually.

> "But behold, that which is of God inviteth and enticeth to do good continually; wherefore, every thing which inviteth and enticeth to do good, and to love God, and to serve him, is inspired of God" (Moroni 7:12-13).

Keep your soul in obedience. It was a cold February night. I had been sleeping soundly under the warm covers of my bed when I came awake with a start. What had first seemed like a dream kept playing across my consciousness until it had awakened me. I listened in the darkness to see if I could determine what had caused my departure from the world of sleep.

A bawling sound came faintly to my ears. I sat up in bed and strained to hear. Although muffled by the walls of the house, the sound was more audible in a sitting position. Something was wrong outside. I jumped out of bed and rushed to the back door, opened it, and listened intently. The sound of one of my calves in distress came clearly to my ears. Although I was barefoot and clad only in my pajamas, the frantic nature of the cry spurred me into immediate action. I sprinted outside, ran to the barn, and followed the sound of the bawling to pen seven.

As I approached the pen I took in the scene with one hurried glance. There, stretched out between two dogs, was one of my bull calves. One dog was biting him on the neck and the other dog was biting him in the flank. As the dogs pulled in opposite directions the calf bellowed in pain and terror. My second observation was as startling as the first. Those were my own dogs, dogs I had trained to be obedient to my commands, and whom I trusted to protect my livestock.

Feeling betrayed, I hurtled the gate and landed on one dog. I picked her up and shot-putted her over the fence. The other dog released his grip on the calf in time to feel my bare toes bury themselves in his ribs. He, too, cleared the fence, but with less velocity. Having disposed of the disobedient dogs, I turned my attention to the wounded calf. I disinfected the lacerations on the calf's neck and side, gave him a shot of antibiotic, and placed him in clean straw in a safe location. Having done all in my power, I left him to heal.

The major purpose for our leaving the cloistered shelter of our premortal home was to prove our obedience to God in an environment of independent decision-making. As we voluntarily choose to keep his commandments, we are blessed according to his promises. As we do his will, we learn empirically that we can always trust him to fulfill his portion of the covenant, and bless us according to the laws we have kept. The challenge we face in mortality is to prove to him that we also can be trusted to fulfill our vows consistently in those circumstances where no one else can supervise or prescribe our actions. For our unrestricted choices to be an agent of upward progression, they must be in concert with his commandments.

After we have securely latched the windows of our minds and locked the doors of our hearts against unwelcome intruders, we must be cautious that we do not reopen our doors to those who knock for fraudulent purposes. If we have developed an ear for the whisperings of the spirit, with equal facility we will recognize the sound of Christ's knock, and his voice will signify to us that we can safely open our doors and admit him into our presence. As we open our hearts to the sound of his voice he will come in to us, and together we will sup on the good fruit of eternal life, which comes to those who love him and keep his commandments.

Chapter 12

If Any of Ye Lack Wisdom

When I was growing up in Tucson, Arizona, I became a Boy Scout at the age of twelve. Ours was a motley patrol, standing out only because of our lack of uniformity. That lack of uniformity extended both to the huge differences in our social-economic backgrounds and to the simple precedent that none of us ever wore a uniform. In fact, the only one who ever did wear a uniform was Mr. Coles, our scoutmaster. Mr. Coles was not a member of the church, but had been recruited for the scoutmaster job because his wife was a member and because nobody else would take it.

Mr. Coles had been a professional boxer when he was younger. While a pugilist, he sustained many concussive blows to his brain. As a consequence of his time in the ring, his mental dexterity was no match for seven mischievous twelve- and thirteen-year-old scouts. His cerebral deficiencies, however, were counterbalanced by his preeminent qualification for the task: he was absolutely fearless. This characteristic was not only necessary for survival but also essential for keeping potential mutineers from jumping ship.

Our scout program consisted of coming to the old Second Ward chapel on Wednesday nights, going to the scout room and tying knots. The following week we would tie knots. The next week we would tie knots. The last week we would play basketball. Of course, when we left scouts we were all knot-heads who didn't unravel when faced with a full court press.

Besides knots and basketball, Mr. Coles taught me another

lesson that has remained with me throughout my life. In our troop were two large-bodied boys who enforced their dominant will because of their size. One of the boys was a Navajo on the Indian Placement program. The other was a kid from a poor home where times were tough and diplomacy was a clenched fist.

Because I was fleet of both tongue and feet it was not difficult to keep these two bullies constantly stirred up and perpetually chasing me. I had fought them individually and in tandem, but fared rather poorly once they threw me to the ground. I discovered that I was more successful when I kept upright and could skip and dodge, and cause them to collide with each other as they attempted to clasp me to them. Mine was a simple tactic, but highly effective as long as I could keep my balance, stay on my feet, and had room to maneuver.

One night before our scout meeting was to start, I had the two of them riled up. Somehow they boxed me into a corner and before I could dance away they worked me over. I looked up from my beating and saw Mr. Coles silently watching us. The next week he brought boxing gloves to our meeting.

Forming a ring in the center of the scout room, he had me strap on a pair of gloves, and then had one of my adversaries don a pair. With the other scouts watching from the edge of the ring, we began circling each other in a menacing fashion. I was half the size of my opponent, but had the advantage of speed and good hand-eye coordination. As we started lobbing fists, I soon realized that my quickness was negated by the smallness of the ring and his superior strength. We stopped to rest after an ineffectual first round and Mr. Coles pulled me aside. Assuming a boxing stance, he placed my left leg in front of my right leg, and then pushed my left arm down below and ahead of my right arm. Then he taught me this fundamental lesson of life in the ring:

"Lead with your left, follow with your right. Use your fists in combination. Jab left, power right. Always use your fists in combination."

This basic principle of boxing is also applicable to our life as saints. Our daily fight with temptations, trials, and adversity is lost when we lob ineffectual fists at our opponents. Only when we use our spiritual gifts as coordinated left-right combinations can we hope to be victorious.

It was just such a left-right combination that struck at the heart of darkness in April of 1820 when a rural, almost illiterate farm boy followed a spiritual prompting to ask God for wisdom because he lacked that precious commodity. He was assured by Holy Writ that if he asked in faith, nothing wavering, he would receive what he asked for. Out of such a simple combination—prayer and faith—emerged the greatest epiphany of all time; a restorative revelation opening the way for a decisive knockout of all that is evil.

As we individually battle the brutes of darkness in this cruel mortal world, we frequently are assailed with opposing stratagems which confuse us and subsequently lower our defenses. It is Satan's ambiguity, and not his directness, that makes him such a cunning, dangerous foe. Like Joseph Smith, we are in dire need of heavenly wisdom to unravel the devilishly clever traps set for us by Lucifer and his minions. As we strike back with the combination of prayer and faith, we receive wisdom from God. Comprehending the difference between God's wisdom and the philosophic wisdom of man is fundamental in the acquisition of Christlike characteristics.

One fine summer day when my children were young and nothing unexpected was ever unexpected, my wife noticed that there was a BB gun bullet hole in our bedroom door. She had a suspect in mind, and when he came prancing through the house a few minutes later she nabbed him by the collar and inquired as to the origin of the hole in the door. Jace, an ultra-free spirit of six years and the new owner of a Daisy Red Rider air rifle, replied in his own defense. "It wasn't me. But if it was me, it was the time my BB gun backfired."

While the word "wise" carries with it many connotations, the generally accepted definition of wisdom is the ability to judge or discern what is true or correct in a matter. Since our ability to gauge the correctness of our actions may be materially affected by our circumstances and experiences, wisdom becomes the product of our environment. If we have immersed ourselves in the ways of the world, then we become worldly-wise when we correctly assess a matter according to societal standards. Because these standards are dynamic in nature and subject to arbitrary change, we may discover that our worldly wisdom is transitory. What is politically correct and socially chic today may be the faux pas of tomorrow.

In stark contrast to the wisdom of the world is God's wisdom. Divine wisdom is based on unchangeable laws and eternal principles, the violation of which brings instant censure from all that is holy. In the Doctrine and Covenants, we are instructed in the difference between worldly wisdom and heavenly wisdom. The promise of divine wisdom is given to those who revere God and serve him.

> *"And their wisdom shall be great, and their understanding reach to heaven; and before them the wisdom of the wise shall perish, and the understanding of the prudent shall come to naught.*
>
> *"For by my Spirit will I enlighten them, and by my power will I make known unto them the secrets of my will—yea, even those things which eye has not seen, nor ear heard, nor yet entered into the heart of man"* (D&C 76:9-10).

As we learn here, godly wisdom extends beyond the boundaries of this earth and reaches to heaven. It cannot be obtained by the worldly expedients of money, social prestige, or even political power. It is received only when the Father's will is clarified through the intelligence-gathering influence of the Holy Ghost.

Because genuine wisdom is such a rare gift, it is much coveted. One of the enticements used by Lucifer to successfully tempt Eve in the Garden of Eden was the promise of wisdom. Solomon was given the gift of wisdom for his righteous desires. The fame of his wisdom was such a powerful enducement to the queen of Sheba that she left her kingdom and traveled many dangerous miles through the Arabian Desert to witness it for herself.

My parents served in the England Manchester Mission during 1989 and 1990. While living in a place called Denton they had their car *pinched*, which is a British colloquialism for *stolen*. This happened four times while they were there. It seems that the young people in the area exercised their entertainment options by breaking the window of a car, hot-wiring it, and going for a joyride.

The first time their car was pinched my parents called the police in great alarm. The constable who came to write their report did not share their anxiety, and predicted that the car would show up when it ran out of petrol. Although the constable was matter-of-fact about obtaining details concerning the stolen car, he waxed almost poetic as he tried to satisfy his curiosity about an American couple living in England.

A few weeks later, my parent's doorbell rang well after midnight. Startled into wakefulness, they stumbled to the door and cautiously opened it. Standing on the threshold was Andy, the constable in charge of their stolen car report. My folks graciously invited him into their flat, although they had no idea why he was there.

Before arriving at their place, Andy had detoured to the local pub where he had attempted to quench his thirst and lubricate his tongue. His thirst was difficult to satisfy, and after an hour of chatting about inconsequential things he suddenly blurted out, "Don't you people ever offer anyone a brew?"

My mother poured him an orange juice, which did not measure up to his liquid-refreshment expectations. Dissatisfied with his beverage, and uncertain that the next one would be more to his liking, he got to the point of his visit. Puzzled about why my parents were living in England, he asked, "Come on now! What's your real reason for being here?"

My father patiently explained that they were missionaries for the Church of Jesus Christ of Latter Day Saints. This simple explanation was apparently incomprehensible to the Englishman's more intricate reasoning, and he countered with the argument that Mormon missionaries were young men in white shirts and ties, not elderly couples with gray hair and grandkids. By this time Andy's tongue was growing a little thick, but he launched into an impassioned tirade about the Mormon Church expecting too much from its members. His church, on the other hand, gave its members great latitude. He could skip church and play golf, or go to the pub, drink his brew, and play darts with his friends. And he could take advantage of all these wonderful activities on Sunday without the smallest pang of compunction. His church even had a vicar who was paid to do the things that the Mormon missionaries went out and did at their own expense. He then challenged my parents to explain such a discrepancy between their church and his church.

It was two a.m. and my mother had had enough. "Because our church isn't for sissies!" she told him.

While much coveted, and openly available to all of God's children, wisdom is not for sissies because it requires us to subjugate undisciplined impulses to the rigor of self-control. Probably the greatest hindrance to acquiring God-given wisdom is this penchant for acquisition without sacrifice or cost. We want something for nothing. We desire God's blessings, but we want them on our terms. We want the knockout, but we want it by throwing one lazy sucker punch, rather than resorting to energy-taxing sparring using effective left-right combinations. In nearly all of Heavenly Father's communications to us, he indicates a combination of forces are necessary to acquire heavenly gifts:

> *"Search diligently, pray always, and be believing, and all things shall work together for your good, if ye walk uprightly and remember the covenant wherewith ye have covenanted one with another"* (D&C 90:24).

> *"Yea, he that repenteth and exerciseth faith, and bringeth forth good works, and prayeth continually without ceasing—unto such it is given to know the mysteries of God. . ."* ((Alma 26:22).

The early American patriot, Thomas Paine, said this: "That which we obtain too easily, we esteem too lightly. It is dearness only which gives everything its value. Heaven knows how to put a proper price on its goods."

Similarly, the Lord has stated his thoughts concerning those who unrealistically expect the windows of heaven to open and pour out a blessing of wisdom when only a minimum of effort is expended.

> *"Behold, you have not understood, you have supposed that I would give it unto you when you took no thought save it was to ask me"* (D&C 9:7).

If we do more than just ask him—if we pray, meditate, study things out in our minds, read the scriptures, walk uprightly, remember our covenants, and exercise our faith—then the Lord will bless us with wisdom. His wisdom will come to us in his own time, and in his own way, and according to his own will.

Once, during my mission, I was in need of wisdom in a hurry. I was being transferred by bus to another part of the mission. During transit a young woman occupying the seat in front of me turned around and inquired whether I was a Mormon missionary. I acknowledged that I was, and we engaged in a conversation about the church. After a time our conversation lagged and she turned back around in her seat. I was left with the disquieting feeling that something was left unspoken that she needed to hear. I prayed silently for wisdom that I might know on what subject I should converse with her. Instantly the words came into my mind, "Baptism for the dead."

As I mulled over the advisability of renewing our discussion with such an unusual lead, the young woman turned toward me and said she had just visited the Washington D.C. Temple (before its dedication). I asked her if she understood our doctrine of eternal marriage and family relationships.

"Yes," she replied, "the only thing I did not understand was your baptizing for the dead."

In this instance, the Lord blessed me with divine wisdom at the juncture where it was necessary. Through the quiet, articulate voice of the Holy Ghost, it was revealed to me what needed to be discussed. Was this bestowal of intelligence for my benefit? No, I already understood the doctrine. Through me the Lord furnished wisdom to a young girl who lacked wisdom.

I had been a bishop for only a short period of time when I received a phone call from a woman in my ward that I had never met. She requested an interview with me for the following Sunday afternoon. Sunday came and was brim-filled with meetings and stressful, emotionally-draining interviews. When this anonymous lady came to the door as the last interview of the day, my most fervent wish was to drop through the floor and somehow reappear in my own home, lying on my own bed. Knowing that my hope was vain, I mentally geared up for one more interview.

The woman entered the office and introduced herself. She was of medium height, had black, unkempt hair, and a blotchy complexion. An aura of gloom surrounded her like a dark cloud. She sat down and began to cry. I handed her a box of Kleenex and settled back in my chair for what appeared to be a marathon session. She began to recite her story:

She was a convert to the church who, after a few years of activity, had committed serious transgression and had been excommunicated from the church. She eventually worked her way past her mistakes and was rebaptized, but had again fallen into inactivity and spiritual lethargy. She had two daughters that she supported; one was mentally retarded and the other suffered from a genetic heart defect. Her life had been a series of personal disasters. Why, she asked, was God doing this to her? Where was His justice? Where was His love? From those initial queries flowed a torrent of other perplexing questions arising from the bitter depths of a woman who felt abandoned by God and His church.

As I quietly listened to this troubled woman, I prayed fervently that I might be able to answer her questions and help her with her problems. While praying, I felt the Spirit of the Lord enter into the room and into my heart. When finally she had concluded her narrative, she requested a blessing. As I laid my hands upon her head the words I was to say came into my mind as though scrolling across a screen. I read them off as they appeared to me. One of the questions that I answered for her in the blessing had been a question that had mystified me since my days as a missionary. It was a profound revelatory experience.

The Lord's wisdom can come to us directly or indirectly, as a receipt of intelligence from the Holy Ghost, or through the inspired words and actions of another person. It may come as an illumination of scripture, or through some resonant chord of truth found in good books. It may come to us at ordinary times in holy places or in ordinary places at times made holy by some stirring of the soul.

When at some forlorn time we think that God has abandoned us or that his wisdom is not forthcoming, we may discover that it has been with us all along. As we drink daily from the living waters of truth, we store reservoirs of wisdom deep within us. On some future day, when it is needed most, we will comprehend the wisdom of God, not on a mental or physical level, but on a deep, soul-touching level that defies description, explanation, or articulation.

Chapter 13

By Small Means

Over fifty years ago, the coral reefs in and around the Carolina Islands in the Pacific Ocean played host to the United States naval fleet. Amongst the carriers and destroyers anchored there was an enormous cargo ship. This ship was anchored off to one side because it carried petroleum in its hold. If an enemy projectile was to penetrate its steel hull, then the explosion had the potential of destroying any vessel within close proximity.

My father was on that cargo ship when they received a report that a squadron of Japanese dive-bombers was headed for the Carolina Islands. The whole fleet immediately sounded the alarm, pulled anchor, and headed out to sea so that they would not be trapped in the reef where they could not maneuver.

On my father's ship, a young officer was ordered to go up and start the engines so that they could depart with the rest of the fleet and be protected by their big guns. In the officer's anxiety to get underway, he turned the motors over too quickly and broke the ship's steering gear. With no way to steer the ship they were like a stationary duck on a pond.

The urgency of the moment created an inventive solution. By running gigantic chains down each side of the boat and attaching them to the rudders, they were able to manually manipulate the direction of sail. By the time they had finished jerry-rigging their ship, three hours had passed, the rest of the fleet had exited, and they were alone in the reef.

As they laboriously crept out toward the open waters of the Pacific, my father was ordered to climb up the mast to the crow's nest, and there keep a vigil for enemy planes. Each anxious moment was filled with fearful anticipation that they would be detected before they could get out to sea and catch up with the rest of the fleet. As they emerged from the reef into the ocean, they spotted a floating dry dock and sailed toward it.

Just then a Japanese dive-bomber dropped out of the clouds and came straight at my father standing in the crow's nest. His warning cry alerted the gunners, and the ship's two small machine guns opened fire in an earnest but ineffectual attempt to defend against the deadly threat of this enemy. The Japanese pilot blithely ignored the small-arms fire, leveled off parallel to the ocean and released his bomb. Fortunately for all aboard, he miscalculated the distance. The bomb sailed over the petroleum cargo and struck the dry dock that exploded in a fiery blast.

A home is like a ship sailing on the ocean. If we stay within the protective cluster of God's proclamations and command- ments, our home becomes a safe sanctuary as we navigate the high seas of life. If we fail to observe divine warnings, then we are left alone to float perilously in enemy waters without means of an effective defense. Too many families disable themselves by hastily jerry-rigging their means of navigation in times of crisis. It cannot be done. We must carefully start the gospel engines in our homes, teaching by both precept and example. Our homes can become a sailing fortress even in troubled waters if we take the necessary precautions.

Joseph Smith was not a sailor, but he gave us some very sound nautical advice:

"You know, brethren, that a very large ship is benefited very much by a very small helm in the time of a storm, by being kept workways with the wind and the waves" (D&C 123:16).

When we speak of crossing the dangerous seas of mortality to the harbor of eternal life, it is the small things that make a large difference in our safely navigating the storms of life.

My father is the inventor of an instrument called a *colostrometer*. The colostrometer is used in the dairy industry to measure the amount of immunoglobulins or antibodies in a cow's first milk. As I mentioned earlier, when a calf is born it has no immunity against disease. By drinking its mother's colostrum it receives a passive immunity that will protect it against disease until its own body can build an active immune system.

Keeping dairy calves alive and free from the debilitating effects of disease is difficult. Expert calf raisers know that there are three small details pertaining to the use of colostrum that will determine both the mortality and morbidity of their calves: First, the colostrum must contain a high level of immunoglobulins. Second, the colostrum must be consumed in large enough quantities to saturate the epithelial cells of the small intestine. Third, the colostrum must be given within the first twelve hours after birth while the cells of the gut are open for antibody absorption. Upon these small factors hinge life or death, sickness or health.

On such small details does our own life often turn. Small Christlike habits, which we have thoughtfully nurtured, may preserve spiritual life and health when temptations weigh heavily upon us. Antithetically, small worldly habits may weigh too heavily against us when spiritual life hangs in the balance. Salvation is measured in these small moments of crisis, when the pull of the flesh is countered by the invitation of the spirit.

No man can serve two masters. As we increase the habits of well-doing we discriminate against the habits of evil-doing. This is as the Lord would have it. Here are his comments set forth in the Doctrine and Covenants:

"Wherefore, be not weary in well-doing, for ye are laying the foundation of a great work. And out of small things proceedeth that which is great" (D&C 64:33).

Mervyn's is my wife's favorite department store. It has been so as long as we have been married, and I suspect it always will remain so. Once, while living in Provo, Laraine had an experience in Mervyn's that cast a shadow upon her shopping enthusiasm.

She was shopping with three small children in tow. My two oldest daughters were three and four years old and ambulatory, while my son was only a year old and in a stroller. Having exhausted all the bargains on the lower floor, it was necessary to ascend to the next level. This movement to a higher kingdom of shopping is simple for a single person, but much more difficult for those souls burdened with little angels.

As my little family approached the escalator, my wife placed the stroller in front of her, stepped on behind it, and hastily instructed my two daughters to follow suit. The two girls were doubtful about the safety of this moving stairway, and stood frozen in place while they watched their mother float to the next level. My wife called down to them to jump on, and gestured emphatically with her free hand to do it now.

By this time a small crowd was beginning to collect behind the girls who were blocking the entrance to the escalator. As my wife moved further away from them, her voice became more emphatic, and her gesticulations more dramatic. A good Samaritan standing behind the girls recognized the dilemma and decided to lend a helping hand. He gently picked up Kodie, my oldest daughter, and attempted to deposit her on the lowest step of the escalator.

This well-intended boost up would certainly have helped the situation except for the fact that Kodie had been well-indoctrinated in the science of *kidnapology*. When a strange man grabbed hold of her, she instinctively resorted to her criminology training. While screaming at an ear-piercing decibel she began to flail away with vicious karate chops and kicks. Her would-be benefactor dropped her, and limped rapidly toward the store exit.

By this time Laraine had reached the top of the escalator and frantically waved to the kids to stay where they were. Having witnessed the destruction of one would-be assistant, no one dared intervene in this intense real-life drama. Instead, they clustered in a fascinated group behind the two kids, waiting nervously to see what scene would unfold next. Their patience was amply rewarded.

With the baby under one arm my wife dashed to the escalator going down. In doing so she disappeared from the sight of the girls. Their already taut nerves could take no more, and bursting into inconsolable sobbing they jumped on the escalator going up. Fortunately, my wife glimpsed them going up as she was going down. She flew down the escalator, and with my son bobbing up and down on her shoulder, sprinted around to the other side. She scaled the escalator steps two at a time and reached the top just as our two hysterical daughters were about to take a descending ride.

In this life there are few big decisions. Instead, there are many small decisions that either take us up or bring us down this moving escalator we call mortality. It is the direction that these accumulated decisions take us, and not the number of decisions made, that ultimately carry us up to celestial heights or down to telestial depths. If we become frightened at the speed we are traveling, or uncertain of the direction, it is prudent to step off our spiritual escalator and orient ourselves to a celestial standard.

As it is in our time, so it was in the days of Nephi. When trials and tribulations came upon Lehi and his family in the wilderness, instead of orienting themselves to celestial standards they accommodated their physical suffering with telestial murmuring. The decisions made during this period of spiritual malaise literally shut down instructions from heaven. The Liahona, which previously had been their compass in the wilderness, refused to work. The family was lost and on the verge of perishing in the desert when Nephi's righteous decisions rescued them from the brink of destruction. A great lesson was taught to the family of Lehi, a lesson that has equal application in our time.

> *"And it came to pass that I, Nephi, beheld the pointers which were in the ball, that they did work according to the faith and diligence and heed which we did give unto them.*
>
> *"And there was also written upon them a new writing, which was plain to be read, which did give us understanding concerning the ways of the Lord; and it was written and changed from time to time, according to the faith and diligence which we gave unto it. And thus we see that by small means the Lord can bring about great things"* (1 Ne. 16:28-29).

My dad grew up on a ranch in Millard County, Utah. One day when he was deacon age, he and his cousin Lloyd George were sent out to look for some missing cattle. As they were about to depart on their search, Raymond Kimball, a friend who lived down the street, brought my father a pair of shotgun chinks and told him that he ought to wear them for his own protection. Although it was an inconvenience, my dad gave heed to the wisdom of his older friend and strapped on the chaps before leaving.

As the two boys rode through the desert area west of

Kanosh, they kept a wary eye out for any sign of the missing animals. The dry desert floor was covered with fine sand and the big thoroughbred mare my dad was riding inadvertently caught her hind leg in a roll of barbed wire that was partially buried by the drifted sand. The rusty wire wrapped around her leg like a trap and tore into her flesh. The mare squealed in pain, and reared straight up in a panicked attempt to rid herself of the barbs digging into her leg.

My father toppled off her back as she reared. As he lay prostrate on the ground the mare frantically stampeded, dragging the wire behind her in the sand. The sharp barbs raked over the top of my father, ripping off his sweater and tearing his chaps into corrugated strips. The chaps were ruined, but their protective covering had spared him serious bodily injury.

In this life, it is these small decisions of faith, taken cumulatively, that protect us from the wires, the waves, and the wilderness, and provide us with a secure compass in a world of great uncertainty. Without spiritual insight to guide our decisions, and without faith to give us the courage to put them in motion, we become a stationary target for hostile and satanic forces to be acted upon before we can act.

Action is the child of decision, and, performed regularly, matures into habit. Habits are the matrix of character, and like our future state of resurrection, some are celestial, some terrestrial, and some telestial. Our decision-making process is first initiated by trial and error, and then becomes materially affected by our daily habits and environment. Eventually our habits and our decisions become part of the same circle, and cause and effect cannot be easily discerned or separated. Unless some outside influence can break the continuity of the cycle, we remain in a state of stasis.

Celestial decisions and actions on an individual level can best be assured if we establish two foundational habits: daily prayer and daily scripture study. Like the Liahona, these basic habits orient us to a celestial standard, and bless our lives with the knowledge, skill, and desire to become like Christ. Opening our spirits to the influence of the divine requires only a small amount of effort on our part. While at times our small daily offering may seem insignificant or even mechanical, repeated regularly and faithfully, prayer and scripture study will inevitably yield a celestial reward.

One who understood this principle was the man Hezekiah. He was twenty-five years old when he became king of Judah, and he reigned for twenty-nine years in the city of Jerusalem. He was of the royal blood of king David and followed the long line of David's descendants that ruled over the split house of Israel. Although he was born into a life of decadence and ease, he differed remarkably from his kingly ancestors. Where his family line trusted in the arm of flesh and the wealth of their royal coffers, Hezekiah trusted implicitly in God, our Heavenly Father. Because of his great faith, the scriptures state that there was none like him before nor none like him after of all the kings of Judah.

Hezekiah understood the law of the Lord, and through prayerful communication he became sensitive to God's will. In his zealousness to do that will, he destroyed all traces of idol worship which was so prevalent in his kingdom. This was a politically unpopular action, for even his forefathers either tacitly or actively participated in the Satan-inspired idolatry.

During the fourth year of the reign of Hezekiah, the Assyrians besieged the northern kingdom of Israel and conquered them after a three-year war. Ten years later, Assyria marched against the kingdom of Judah, and captured all her cities except Jerusalem. Before attacking fortified Jerusalem, king Sennacherib of Assyria sent a delegation of ambassadors into the city to frighten the people into surrender. These skilled saboteurs spread propaganda regarding the invincibility of the mighty Assyrian army. Hezekiah countered with this simple message: have faith in God, he will deliver us.

At this critical juncture, Hezekiah retreated to the temple and there sought the Lord in prayer. At the same time he sent messengers to the prophet Isaiah seeking counsel from the Lord's living oracle. Isaiah's return message was not to fear the blustering words of the Assyrians, for the Lord God would deliver Judah.

Soon thereafter, the Assyrian's bellicose intentions were diverted by enemy eruptions in Libnah, and Ethiopia. As the Assyrians abandoned their siege of Jerusalem, they sent correspondence to king Hezekiah that he shouldn't get too comfortable because of his temporary reprieve. They would be back.

Even after the threat of an imminent Assyrian conquest was gone, Hezekiah continued to petition the Lord in fervent prayer. His faithful prayers were heard and answered. Through the prophet Isaiah, Hezekiah was instructed that no matter how colossal the Assyrian power appeared to be, it was of no significance when compared to the power of God. The king of Assyria would never enter Jerusalem. That promise was to be fulfilled miraculously.

After King Sennacherib smashed the insurgency in his far-flung kingdom, the Assyrians once more turned their predatory attention toward Jerusalem. As the huge Assyrian army camped on their return march, the angel of the Lord visited their encampment and killed 185,000 soldiers. When king Sennacherib awoke the next morning he was horrified to discover that his army had been destroyed during the night. Unprotected by his massive army, he retreated to the city of Nineveh where he was murdered by his own sons.

As it was in Hezekiah's time, so it is in our time. The battle against evil is ongoing. Satan and his ambassadors continue to hector us into believing that resistance is futile, that defeat is inevitable, that the odds of victory are so miniscule as to be incalculable. In answer to such compelling propaganda we turn to the words of the prophet Alma:

> *"Now ye may suppose that this is foolishness in me; but behold I say unto you, that by small and simple things are great things brought to pass; and small means in many instances doth confound the wise.*
>
> *"And the Lord God doth work by means to bring about his great and eternal purposes; and by very small means the Lord doth confound the wise and bringeth about the salvation of many souls"* (Alma 37:6-7).

Despite the blustering influence of the devil, despite the popular social philosophies of the day, Alma's words give us resolve to continue to pursue those small things necessary for our salvation and the salvation of our children. Taken singly, simple acts of goodness and small teachings of righteousness may seem like insignificant trickles of water in a parched and thirsty desert. But taken together, these small and simple actions will flood the world with goodness, and the desert shall blossom as a rose.

Chapter 14

Meek And Lowly Of Heart

While going to school at the University of Arizona in Tucson, I worked as a valet at Skyline Country Club to support my family. One night I was stationed outside the clubhouse to wait for diners to come out and claim their cars. As I waited, I closely observed the interior of the building through two port windows mounted in the front door. My watch was rewarded when I spied a man and a woman enter from the dining room and proceed toward me at the exit.

The couple's forward progress suddenly halted, and I could see that they were engaged in argument. Without warning, the woman suddenly slapped her male companion. Before the astonished man could recover and defend himself, his lady companion administered six more staccato blows to his face. The man finally recovered his balance, cocked his right arm, and delivered a devastating wallop to the woman's jaw. The woman momentarily elevated off the ground and then crumpled to the floor.

I rushed into the building and separated the two combatants. A security officer was soon at my side and pushed the man into a corner. I assisted the woman off the floor and examined her face for injury. The jaw was reddened but apparently intact. There was no injury to her tongue, and it was soon moving at an alarming speed. Her vociferous scolding carried throughout the country club as she rebuked her husband for whacking her in the face and failing to complete his expensive dinner. It was obvious that water had not been the beverage of choice with dinner.

As this violent domestic incident illustrates, a father who leads with an angry right can't expect his family to come out standing. Compare his foolish behavior with the type of behavior the Lord expects us to adopt.

"No power or influence can or ought to be maintained by virtue of the priesthood, only by persuasion, by long-suffering, by gentleness and meekness, and by love unfeigned. . ." (D&C 121:41).

In the last week of Jesus' mortal life, as he entered Jerusalem for what would be the final time, the people of Judea thronged the streets casting down palm fronds and articles of clothing in his path. They clamored for a Messiah, a powerful king to rise up and topple the political hegemony of Roman rule off Jewish backs. In stark contrast to the people's expectations, the Savior of the world requested a young donkey that he might fulfill this prophecy:

". . .Behold, thy King cometh unto thee, meek, and sitting upon an ass. . ." (Matthew 21:5).

In his final earthly hours, the preeminent characteristic of the Savior was his meekness—a characteristic that he enjoins all his disciples to emulate:

"Come unto me, all ye that labour and are heavily laden, and I will give you rest.
"Take my yoke upon you, and learn of me; for I am meek and lowly of heart: and ye shall find rest unto your souls" (Matthew 11:28-29).

Jesus, our Lord and Savior, was the most forceful and dynamic personality who ever lived. How is it possible that a man of such enormous spiritual and physical vitality could also be meek and lowly of heart? Does his meekness pose a spiritual paradox or does it show a misunderstanding on our part of the true nature of this attribute?

I had been out on my mission for less than a month when our district set up a booth in a shopping mall in Hampton, Virginia. It was Christmastime and the mall was a scene of perpetual motion. Amidst this activity, we stood behind our booth answering questions from passing shoppers.

At one point I was left in the booth with another neophyte missionary. Elder Cowley was a farmer's son from rural Utah, and had arrived in the mission field the same day I had. He had curly brown hair, a wide infectious grin, and spoke a peculiar southern Utah dialect.

While in the mission home in Salt Lake City, we had seen a movie concerning Christ in the Americas, and about the archeological findings involving pre-Columbian Christian worship. The film had been narrated by a BYU archeologist who instilled in the production both an intellectual and spiritual aura. It had left a deep impression on me, and (I soon learned) on Elder Cowley as well.

While we manned the booth together, we were approached by a born-again Southern Baptist gentleman. Without prelude, he launched a vehement attack on the wicked and false doctrines of the Mormon cult. Pedestrian traffic slowed as curious shoppers craned their necks to see what the excitement was about. I tried to reason with the man on a rational level, but soon recognized the futility of the assignment and gave it up. My companion, however, had grown up on the farm and knew the importance of sticking with a task.

As the man continued to rail against the church, Elder Cowley grew increasingly incensed. His face flushed, his nostrils distended, and his eyes glowed with an ardor I had never witnessed before. Each criticism from our antagonist was met by a spirited reply. Finally the man made one last damning remark and then turned to go. Elder Cowley would not allow him the satisfaction of leaving the battlefield having fired the parting shot, and lobbed this verbal grenade at the man's retreating back:

"I know the Mormon Church is true because it was proved by architects!"

The man half-turned, gave us a quizzical look, and then rushed off shaking his head. Elder Cowley grinned triumphantly at me. In his moment of victory, I did not have the heart to define the difference between architects and archeologists.

> *"And again, behold I say unto you that he cannot have faith and hope, save he shall be meek, and lowly of heart.*
>
> *"If so, his faith and hope is vain, for none is acceptable before God, save the meek, and lowly of heart;..."*
> (Moroni 7:43-44).

With so much at stake, we cannot afford to misinterpret the defining characteristics of this essential Christ-like attribute. Our cursory understanding of meekness may have more to do with how the word sounds and the connotations placed on it by worldly standards than actual fact.

While my children were young, it was my habit to awaken them early in the morning to get ready for school. One morning I began rubbing my nine-year-old daughter's back and telling her how wonderful it was to be able to wake up bright and early.

Riki turned over and said, "Dad, you are weird!"

I replied, "That's only a condition of your mind, only your perception of me. After all, my weird might be normal."

"All right," she retorted, "you're normally weird!"

The world's normal perception of the meek is of spiritless, timid, submissive souls easily duped and imposed upon. As Latter-day Saints our view of meekness might be considered weird when compared to commonly-held perceptions. While we consider the meek to be submissive, it is to God's will that they submit. To be meek and lowly of heart means that we subordinate our imperfect desires for the greater good that derives from subjection to the perfect will of the Father. As always, our great exemplar is our elder brother Jesus:

> "Learn of me, and listen to my words; walk in the meekness of my Spirit, and you shall have peace in me.
> "I am Jesus Christ; I came by the will of the Father, and I do his will" (D&C 19:23-24).

Contrary to publicly-held perceptions, the meek are not fearful and spineless. Instead, the meek are the most courageous people on earth. They are the god-fearing and righteous who willingly conform to gospel standards regardless of the popularity of their position or the opposition to those standards. Thus, we can say with equal propriety, that Jesus exhibited his meekness not only when he quietly submitted himself to the indignity of the cross, but also when he dramatically drove the moneychangers from the temple. Meekness, in its richest gospel sense, is akin to consecration and not trepidation.

Lyman Wight was an early convert to the church and eventually an apostle. When the saints were driven out of their homes in Jackson County, Missouri, someone needed to report the situation to the prophet Joseph in Kirkland, Ohio. Because of the extreme danger in traveling through Missouri as a member of the church, volunteers were scarce. Lyman Wight volunteered to make the trip. Leaving his wife by the side of a log in the woods with a three-day-old baby and provisions for only three days, he undertook this dangerous assignment. He had faith that if he did the will of the Lord, the Lord would take care of his family.

During later Missouri persecutions, Lyman Wight was imprisoned with Joseph Smith and several other leading brethren. While incarcerated, Brigadier General Moses Wilson of the opposing mob militia offered him any political appointment in the state of Missouri if he would give written testimony against Joseph Smith. The alternative was execution. Lyman Wight answered this way:

"General, you are entirely mistaken in your man, both in regards to Joseph Smith and myself. Joseph Smith is not an enemy to mankind, he is not your enemy, and is as good a friend as you have got. Had it not been for him, you would have been in hell long ago, for I would have sent you there. And no other man than Joseph Smith could have prevented me, and you may thank him for your life."

General Wilson replied, "Wight, you are a strange man; but if you will not accept my proposal you will be shot tomorrow morning at eight."

Lyman Wight's reply: "Shoot and be damned."

To the meek, consecration of time, talents, and life is readily placed on the altar of duty if we are assured that it is God's will. Integral to the acquisition of meekness is the understanding of what is, in fact, God's will. Too frequently we misunderstood the mind of our Heavenly Father, allocating to his will our own desires and inclinations. While often our desires may spring from righteous intent, still, failure to distinguish between God's actual will and what we want his will to be demonstrates spiritual indolence and irresponsibility on our part.

> *"For my thoughts are not your thoughts, neither are your ways my ways, saith the Lord.*
>
> *"For as the heavens are higher than the earth, so are my ways higher than your ways, and my thoughts than your thoughts"* (Isaiah 55:8-9).

The key to discerning between our will, man's will, Satan's will, and God's will, is prayer.

"But ye are commanded in all things to ask of God, who giveth liberally; and that which the Spirit testifies unto you even so I would that ye should do in all holiness of heart, walking uprightly before me, considering the end of your salvation, doing all things with prayer and thanksgiving, that ye may not be seduced by evil spirits, or doctrines of devils, or the commandments of men; for some are of men, and others of devils" (D&C 46:7).

"He that asketh in the Spirit asketh according to the will of God; wherefore it is done even as he asketh" (D&C 46:30).

It is apparent that we cannot act meekly or acquire the characteristic of meekness unless we are in tune with the Spirit through prayer.

When my son Jace was a six-year-old, he and two of his buddies kept things stirred up in their Primary class. One Sunday his Primary teacher complained to my wife that Jace was being raucously loud in class. Later that day Laraine asked Jace how he had behaved during Primary. "Oh, pretty good," he replied nonchalantly. My wife explained that his teacher had offered a contrary opinion and that perhaps the two of them differed in what they thought good behavior was supposed to be. She followed that comment with the subtle threat that perhaps she should check with his teacher every week to see how he was behaving in class. Jace thought about that for a second and then said, "That's a good idea, Mom. Then I can tell you when she's lying."

Occasionally we need to check up on ourselves to see how we are doing. As we become truly meek we may notice new behavioral patterns emerging in our lives. The prophet Mormon explains that we must be meek and lowly of heart before we can acquire the gift of charity. Those who are charitable act with love and righteous intent toward their fellowman. They comport themselves in a kind, patient, nonjudgmental manner toward others, rejoicing with them in their successes, bearing with them in their failures and frailties of body and spirit. With such a celestial attitude toward others, it is no wonder that the meek will inherit the earth in its sanctified state.

When I was a boy I loved baseball with a passion. I practiced it and played it at every opportunity. What every aspiring ball player needs is a good glove, and I wanted my own baseball mitt more than anything else in the world. I supplicated my parents for a glove, but finances were tight and my importuning produced only a stirring of sympathy. By the time I was eight years old I was certain that I was the most under-privileged kid on the planet.

Finally, when I was convinced that I would travel through life gloveless, a miracle occurred. My mother had been saving Gold Bond trading stamps from her grocery purchases. One day she took stock of the Gold Bond books she had filled and discovered that it was a sizable collection. In those days stamp books could be redeemed at special stores for free gifts. My mom charitably informed me that I could trade her Gold Bond books for a baseball mitt.

I remember walking into the store and being transported to paradise. I pranced to the sporting goods department unable to contain my excitement. My dad stopped at the baseball equipment aisle, stretched an arm to a top shelf, and pulled down a box with a Wilson insignia on it. He handed the box to me. I sat down on the floor and carefully opened it up. Inside was a sleek leather glove autographed by Larry Sherry. It was a dream come true. Outside the store, I climbed back in the car, sniffed the rich new leather, pounded the glove with my fist, and pretended to catch an imaginary fly ball. Life didn't get any better than this.

My Wilson glove was my pride and joy, and I eagerly showed it off to my friends. Some of the more sage baseballers amongst them informed me that I needed to break it in properly by oiling it. Not wanting to appear ignorant, I nodded my head wisely, and then went home and tried to puzzle out what type of oil I was supposed to use. I looked around the place.

The only two oils I could find were motor oil and Crisco vegetable oil; the one seemed too harsh and the other too greasy. I was running out of options when I remembered that in the kitchen cupboard was a large glass bottle marked olive oil. I knew that my dad sometimes used the oil to give blessings to the sick, and figured that if it was good enough for that purpose it was good enough for the best baseball glove a boy could ever have. I took the olive oil down from the cupboard and applied it to the new leather. It imparted a very unique odor to my mitt, and changed the color of the leather from a light tan to a dark chocolate.

For the next several years I used that glove. It saw me through Little League, Pony League, and right up to high school. During that time I continued to preserve the leather with consecrated olive oil. By the time I retired my Larry Sherry autographed model it was a dark, dark black in color, and carried with it a pungent, rancid aroma that could be identified from shortstop to first base if a light breeze was blowing. No one ever attempted to steal my glove, and no one ever, ever asked to borrow it.

Like my Wilson baseball glove, meekness is not a free gift, but one that is gained only after long strugglings and much solicitation of the spirit. It is a gift that must be taken care of assiduously, oiling it often with our best consecrated labors. It is a gift that must be acquired honestly, for it cannot be borrowed, and it cannot be stolen.

The prophet Mormon knew of the importance of this divine

characteristic, and imparted his knowledge of its acquisition to his son Moroni.

"And the first fruits of repentance is baptism; and baptism cometh by faith unto the fulfilling the commandments; and the fulfilling the commandments bringeth remission of sins;

"And the remission of sins bringeth meekness, and lowliness of heart; and because of meekness and lowliness of heart cometh the visitation of the Holy Ghost, which Comforter filleth with hope and perfect love, which love endureth by diligence unto prayer, until the end shall come, when all the saints shall dwell with God" (Moroni 8:25-26).

As we diligently strive for this most fundamental of Christlike virtues, we will witness the spiritual fulfillment of his words to us. To the meek and lowly of heart the yoke of discipleship is easy, and the burden of the gospel is light.

Chapter 15

Open Windows

My high school baseball coach was Bobby "Sparrow-legs" Hart. Sparrow Hart made quite a name for himself in Arizona athletics during the late 1940's when he starred for Amphitheatre High School in Tucson. He quarterbacked the football team, played guard on the basketball team, pitched for the baseball team, and ran the hurdles in track.

Despite his many athletic accomplishments, Sparrow Hart's claim to fame was established while he waited for a basketball game to start. Amphitheatre High had qualified for a basketball tournament in Phoenix, and since the tournament would last for two days, the team was quartered at a local motel with two players to a room. Sparrow Hart was assigned a room with the star player on the team, a tall forward who was a gifted scorer.

After an exhausting morning game, the players retired to their motel rooms to rest for the evening's contest. Sparrow Hart had an errand to run and did not return immediately to his room. When he did come in, he discovered that his room-mate was sleeping soundly in the bathtub. Sparrow was not an evil person, but he was subject to temptation. He left the motel room, hustled across the street to a drug store, and returned carrying a bottle of blue india ink. He carefully emptied the bottle of ink into the bathtub, stirred the contents gently, and closed the door quietly as he left. For another half hour the star player slept blissfully while he underwent a most remarkable transformation.

Later that evening the game began as scheduled. The stands were crowded with fans looking for high-quality entertainment and college scouts looking for blue-chip prospects. Thanks to Sparrow Hart they both got what they paid for. That night Amphitheatre's forward seemed to flow all over the court. He was as smooth as ink as he made his signature moves underneath the basket, and put his stamp on the game. Everyone who witnessed his performance was impressed—indelibly.

One of the most remarkable visions ever recorded in scripture, and one that should be outlined in blue ink and indelibly impressed upon our minds, is found recorded in the book of Abraham. Using the Urim and Thummim, the seer Abraham learned the relationship of earth to heaven, and man to God. Like a window opening to heaven, Abraham saw our premortal relationships, and learned the purpose of our mortal existence.

> *"And there stood one among them that was like unto God, and he said unto those who were with him: We will go down, for there is space there, and we will take of these materials, and we will make an earth whereon these may dwell;*
>
> *"And we will prove them herewith, to see if they will do all things whatsoever the Lord their God shall command them;*
>
> *"And they who keep their first estate shall be added upon; and they who keep not their first estate shall not have glory in the same kingdom with those who keep their first estate; and they who keep their second estate shall have glory added upon their heads for ever and ever"* (Abraham 3:24-26).

A *principle* is a fundamental standard of truth used for measuring conduct. The principle of obedience is the Lord's gauge for determining our desire to become like him and is fundamental in our quest for eternal progression.

Commandments are given as a means to prove our obedience and make up that canon of doctrine considered *gospel law*. To every law that we obey there is an attached blessing. The attached blessing comes in the form of progression toward Godliness and is so intimately intertwined with the commandment that its realization is instantaneous with our willing submission to the law. We progress toward Godliness at the rate we comply with the commandments and master the principle of obedience. In stark contrast, the consequence of disobedience is the lack of progression toward Godliness and the corresponding reduction of Christlike characteristics.

Embodying the spirit of all the commandments, the Lord gives us this challenge to our divine progression:

> *"Wherefore, I give unto them a commandment, saying thus: Thou shalt love the Lord thy God with all thy heart, with all thy might, mind, and strength: and in the name of Jesus Christ thou shalt serve him"* (D&C 59:5).

In 1983 my father retired from the University of Arizona and purchased a small ranch in Letha, Idaho. I flew down to Tucson from my home in Utah to help my parents move up. After a three-day trip we arrived at the ranch, and were met there by my sister Merry. The house had been rented out for several years, but was now unoccupied and awaited its new tenant. As we entered the old home our nostrils were immediately assailed by the putrefying aroma of a dead animal. Holding our noses, we tiptoed across the living room floor and felt it sag beneath our feet. The walls looked tired, and seemed to droop under the burden of holding up the roof. The bathroom sink was a heap of rubble, having collapsed on its own volition. Everything was filthy; every room smelled musty. The house seemed to say, "leave me alone, I've suffered enough."

My sister and I came to the same independent conclusion. My parents should level the house and start over. We expressed our opinion. No, my folks replied, we will restore, and clean, and refurbish, and make this place better than it ever was. I flew back to Utah with serious misgivings concerning my parents' sanity.

Several months later I returned for a visit. At great expense and sacrifice, the house had been miraculously transformed by the labors of many skilled professionals working together as a harmonious team. The walls had been strengthened, the foundation propped up, the interior gutted and renewed. The fresh smell of carpet and paint had replaced the fetid odor of dead cat. Everywhere I looked was order and cleanliness. The home was now unique in its style and attractive inside and out. The work of salvation was complete.

Our physical body houses the spirit, and is sometimes referred to as our tabernacle. The soul is comprised of the body and the spirit. The body listens to the elements of the carnal world and is subject to the cravings of the natural man. The spirit is educated in the ways of God our Father, and is sensitive to truths learned in the premortal existence. For those who live a life dedicated to the whims and impulses of the natural man, their tabernacles reflect a dissolute and spiritually-neglected frame. Our eventual salvation depends upon whether we are able to maintain a tabernacle that responds to the restoring corrections of the spirit.

The salvational work on our soul is generally a work in progress, and is not complete until after much renovation. As we build our love for our Heavenly Father by diligently serving him in the name of Jesus Christ, our spiritual foundation gradually becomes strong and secure, our walls firm and unyielding, and our rooms clean and orderly. At this point in our progression we eagerly look forward to a final inspection of our labors, and a pronouncement of approval from our Savior. As we feel his love, and hear the phrase "well done, thou good and faithful servant," then we will know that we have merited an inheritance with him in the mansions of our Father.

About the Author

Kevin Stott was born in Madison, Wisconsin, and was raised in Tucson, Arizona.

After attending a year of college at Brigham Young University, he served a mission for the LDS Church in Virginia. He then returned to BYU and met Laraine Graf, who he married in 1977.

Kevin transferred to the University of Arizona, where he graduated with a degree in Animal Science in 1980. He has since worked as an independent dairy nutritional consultant in Utah and Idaho.

Kevin and Laraine are the parents of two sons and three daughters. He has served in various positions within the LDS Church, and is currently serving in the Emmett Idaho Stake presidency. His hobbies involve horses, dogs, and any reason to be outdoors.